# Sculptural Ceramics

# Sculptural Ceramics

Ian Gregory

A&C Black · London
Chilton Book Company · Radnor, Pennsylvania

First published in Great Britain 1992
A & C Black (Publishers) Limited
35 Bedford Row, London WC1R 4JH

ISBN 0–7136–3580–0

A CIP catalogue record for this book is available from
the British Library

First published in USA by Chilton Book Company, Radnor,
Pennsylvania 19089.

ISBN 0–8019–8387–8

*Jacket illustrations*:
*front*:  Left – Torso by the Author. Stoneware with coiled T-
           material, coiled and stained with oxides, matt turquoise
           glaze. Height – 4'6".
           Top right – 'The Lion Tamer's Daughter' by Michael Flynn.
           Raku. Height – 60".
           Bottom right – 'Violets' by Peter Simpson. Biscuit slips,
           alkaline glazes, fired at 1240°C, polished and lacquered.
*Back*:   Female figure by Donna Polseno. Earthenware, coiled,
           stained slips, fluxed with Gerstley borates.

*Frontispiece*: 'Meditation' by Ian Gregory. Life size.
Coiled, craft crank, fired at 1220°C in light reduction.

Filmset by Florencetype Ltd, Kewstoke, Avon.
Printed by Butler & Tanner Ltd, Frome, Somerset

# Contents

# Acknowledgements

Initially when I set out to write this book it seemed a simple task, setting down the relevant information on various techniques in a direct order of materials and making methods. There is, however, so much more information that relates to each of the specialised areas that it is not possible to go into them in depth in this one volume. The basic principles are here as a guide for further investigation by the individual in whichever technique he is interested in. There have also had to be omissions for similar reasons with regard to some of the more specialised techniques.

There is so much interesting work being made at this present time by a great diversity of artists both in this country and abroad, that there are many that have not been included amongst the illustrations. Only a general cross-section is shown; hopefully they are representative of the genre as a whole.

I would like to take this opportunity to thank all those who found the time to answer my letters and send such a wealth of material both written and visual and without whose generous help it would not have been possible to produce this book.

My thanks must also go to my editor, Linda Lambert, for her help and encouragement, to Charles Cowling for his guidance in the use of the word processor, to Clare Gregory and Thomas Gregory for their help on the sidelines and, not least, to Lynda Muir for her constant support and help both during the writing of the text and photography of some of the making methods.

Finally, my thanks to the following artists and photographers who have kindly allowed me to include their work in this book: Jeff Mincham, Grant Hancock, David Scott, Alison Britton, John Maltby, Michael Flynn, Richard Slee, Gordon Baldwin, Stephen Brayne, Christie Brown, Michel Kuipers, Mo Jupp, Paul Astbury, Gillian Lowndes, Ruth Barrett-Danes, Philip Eglin, Angus Suttie, T. Hill, David Miller, Gary Wornell, Anna Lambert, Delan Cookson, Eileen Lewenstein, Alan Wallwork, John Neely, Greg Daly, Tina Vlassopulos, Sharon Blakey, Peter Beard, Sarah Gregory, Bill McNamara, Esperanza Romero, Russell Coates, Jim Robison, Colin Kellam, Dorothy Feibleman, Svend Bayer, Sandy Brown, Anne Mercer, Pamela Mei-Yee Leung, Helen Ridehalgh, Mark Tomlinson, Rachel Gregory, Tony Deane, David Cripps, Michael Bayley, Thomas Ward, Jutka Fisher, Andrew Morris, John Kershaw, Sebastian Blackie, Anthony Theakston, Monica Young, Colin Pearson, Peter Phillips, Mark Stanczyk, Paul Soldner, Mark Tomlinson, Barbara Tipton, Laurie Spencer, Vincent McGrath, Donna Polseno, David Suckling, Peter Simpson, Nickolas Gossip, Irene Vonk, Ken Eastman, Jill Crowley, Kate Malone, John Chalke, David Vandekop, Vladimir Tsivin, Sarah Scampton, and Xavier Toubes.

'Two women chatting'. Made at Myrrina in Asia Minor, 100BC.
*British Museum*

# Introduction

*'Eternity is in love with the products of time.'*
*William Blake*

There is an enormous variety and range in the ceramics being created today. The work produced is rich in visual imagery, reflecting a multitude of social and cultural influences at work. The ceramics range in size from small domestic pieces that can be enjoyed in the home or a gallery environment to the larger and perhaps more challenging pieces that are in private and public collections in the open air. They are all the products of the hand and eye, and that inner drive of the artist who conceives them. All are the expression of the need to communicate to others through a three-dimensional image.

All of the artists depicted in this book have moved away from the constraints of earlier, more traditional, influences and have sought to express themselves in new and innovative ways. They have developed their own unique styles through their exploration of ideas and their understanding of the clays, glazes and firing methods within whichever temperature range thay have chosen to work. In some cases they have elected to use mixed media with their ceramics to achieve their desired results. This does not mean that the work is essentially no longer within the context of ceramics. Instead it shows an openness to finding new ways to develop ideas that push boundaries forward or to establish fresh solutions to old problems.

Whatever the source, motivation or inspiration, all work must inevitably be judged on its own merit. Good art will always remain timeless, with its roots firmly in the amorphous folk art of the past and yet still belonging to and reflecting the experiences of its own time. I feel that the work shown in this book meets these criteria.

Today there is an awareness of the potter and his work that was not there 40 or 50 years ago. The change came about in the 1960s and 1970s, and this new popularity, whatever its basis, has created an atmosphere which has allowed potters to flourish. As an awareness and appreciation for their work has developed so too has their striving to find new forms of expression that show a sensitivity and integral understanding of their materials. The result has been some truly outstanding and innovative work.

In this book I am going to discuss handbuilt sculptural ceramics, looking first at historical examples, then discussing the techniques and materials used when handbuilding and finally taking a look at what is currently being done in the field. I hope within these pages there will be something to appeal to every taste and be representative of the rich diversity of objects that are being produced in the present free climate of self-expression.

# A Brief History of Sculptural Ceramics

**M**an has created images in clay almost from the beginning of his existence. The diversity of examples from every culture on our planet fill museums and ceramic collections around the world. Here are included just a few examples to show the historical pedigree of ceramic works and to illustrate the deep need that mankind seems to have to give its imagination and artistic drive a tangible reality.

The long history of ceramics both as vessels and decorative or votive objects has enriched lives throughout the ages and allows us today a glimpse of the needs and aspirations of past societies. Interestingly, though the vessel has been in use for many thousands of years, the clay image dates back even further. Since the dawn of time, man seems to have had a drive to externalise himself by reproducing three-dimensional interpretations of either animals or himself. This is shown in the small effigies particularly of fertility goddesses in human form that were produced by some early tribal societies. Many of the forms were refined over and over, reducing the shapes and decoration to their very essence so that there no longer remained any separation between the relationship of form and pattern.

In using the tactile medium of clay the maker's sensitivity to form and texture and his ability to manipulate the interrelating shapes either complex or simple are governed by the intellect as well as intuition. Line and shape, the weight or containment of space, the relationship of one surface to another, balance and harmony are all essential ingredients in what is almost a language of clay. When these combine together they produce an aesthetic quality which we are able to respond to whether the object was made yesterday or ten thousand years ago.

Progress has not always followed a particular pattern from one culture to another. The materials available, the kiln technology and the cultural perception of the wares and decoration needed all played their part in the development of the ceramic art. For instance, in the Middle

Fertility goddess. Female figure in terracotta. Taxilia, 2,000–3,000BC.
*Courtesy of the Trustees of the Victoria and Albert Museum.*

East in neolithic times, items were made using a basic red earthenware clay with slip decoration. Later (around 2000 BC) these potters developed simple glazes though their kiln technology remained fairly primitive. However, at about the same time, Chinese potters were producing harder stonewares with more sophisticated glazes. The ability to produce these effects came about because of the Chinese love of bronze work. The Chinese metal workers had developed large, high-firing furnaces for their smelting work and the potters adopted this

Pottery warrior figures of Han tomb on display in Xianyang Museum.
*Xinhua News Agency.*

Chinese horse. Unglazed, grey earthenware. 6th Dynasty.
*Courtesy of the Trustees of the Victoria and Albert Museum.*

technology for their pots. Indeed, the adoption of the large furnaces meant that they could also fire large ceramic pieces. This is strikingly shown in the 'Emperor's warrior army' which has recently been found at Mount Li in China.

Chinese cultural requirements also shaped the development of their ceramics. Jade was a highly valued commodity in ancient China and potters emulated its lovely green grey colour in their celadon glazes which were used on domestic and votive objects as well as moulded roof tiles, decorative friezes and other architectural ornamentation. Similarly, during the Tang dynasty when an edict was passed that wives and servants no longer needed to be buried with their dead husbands, there grew up a tradition of making copies of goods and chattels to be carried with the dead into the after life. This produced an unsurpassed number of exquisitely modelled animals, statuettes and portraits of household officials and retainers.

9

## Other Early Developments

### Romans and Greeks

The Romans and Greeks also developed sophisticated firing techniques which allowed them greater freedom in producing both small statuettes and their monumental tomb figures and sarcophagi. They also developed elaborate means of ornamentation. These are clearly shown in the relief figures and complex images which appear on the surfaces of much of their work. (See photograph below.)

Etruscan sarcophagi. Terracotta.
*British Museum*

Nok head from Nigeria, 500BC–220AD.
*Nigerian National Commission for Museums and Monuments.*

### Central American Indians (AD 950 onwards)

In Mexico, the Mayas used friezes depicting domestic and wild animals intermixed with calligraphic symbols to decorate their temples. Their smaller pieces often used the same images and they have a strong and assertive feeling even today.

Much earlier, the Zapotec Indians had produced large funeral urns in the form of animals and gods. These can stand on their own both as works of art as well as being containers for bodily remains.

## Later European Developments

In Europe ceramic wares continued to develop, spurred on, as trading links grew, by the importation of wares from other countries. The Moors introduced tin glazed earthenware from the Middle East into Spain where it became known as maiolica. The technique in turn travelled to Italy where it was further modified and called faience, and then on to the Netherlands where Delftware was created and to England where a number of wares including Lambethware appeared.

Probably of greatest influence though were the Chinese ceramics which began to arrive in quantity in Europe during the 16th, 17th and 18th centuries. They were highly prized and European potteries developed ever more sophisticated methods and technologies in order to imitate these Chinese wares. For instance, great efforts were made to perfect fine porcelain. The French became renowned for this type of work which was initially produced in Vincennes. Their figurines were Baroque in style and light and elegant. Later developments included extremely decorative panels which were set into

Tureen and cover with sculpted features.
Hard paste porcelain. Sevres, *c.* 1775.
*Courtesy of the Trustees of the Victoria and Albert Museum.*

furniture and used as wall panels. The factories of Sèvres and Limoges competed against one another in the production of both soft and hard porcelain and an abundance of ornamental work was produced.

Capodimonte had factories in both Italy and Spain. They used a soft Italian paste which could be modelled into very thin translucent forms, rococo and flamboyant, for which they became famous. The Capodimonte were very much

Pair of parrots with purple breasts.
Meissen, *c.* 1740.
*Courtesy of the Trustees of the Victoria and Albert Museum.*

influenced by the Meissen wares which were imported from Germany.

There were many ceramic factories in Germany among which the ones in Meissen were most famous. The German factories used a paste that was quite hard and more closely resembled the Chinese high-fired porcelains that were so much admired. Gottlieb Kirchner and other sculptors made life-size figures of animals and birds for the Meissen factories and these remain some of the finest examples of modelling in this material to be found.

In England, earthenware remained the basic material from which most ceramics were fashioned. This was mostly due to the abundance of good local clays available around the country. There was imitation of Chinese decorative styles but there also remained a strong domestic tradition, many fine examples of which can still be

seen today. Then in the 1670s John Dwight introduced and developed the use of salt glazed stonewares copied from German methods of production. This in turn encouraged higher firing bodies. This was a time of great experimentation for the potters. Clays were combined to produce a variety of wares and glazes, lustres and enamels were used to highlight the forms and relief on many pieces.

The advent of the Industrial Revolution heralded a period of enormous change for the potteries. Mass production came to the fore and large factories sprang up, taking the place of many of the smaller traditional workshops. This change demanded the development both of new working methods and new materials such as Staffordshire creamware and the porcelains of

Worcester and Derby. An enormous amount of ceramic items were now produced. These ranged from tableware to small decorative pieces to highly popular tiles and architectural murals as well as statues and other sculptural items.

## North America

In the New England colonies there was also a tradition of using red earthenware and gradually, as elsewhere, new technology was introduced as European immigrants brought their expertise with them. Stoneware production was started in the area of New York where there was an ample supply of high-firing clays. Salt glazing was begun there and in other parts of the country where the necessary materials were available. Also, at much the same time as their European counterparts, American potteries began to develop porcelain mixtures that were of a very high quality. They used their version of Parian ware to make a range of figurative pieces based on popular motifs and busts of famous characters. The porcelain factories also produced very Baroque modelled dishes which depicted flora and fauna of every type. The American Civil War forced some of these porcelain factories to stop production and by the time the war had ended, tastes had changed and there wasn't as much demand for their wares. Instead, country pottery became popular again and the production of three-dimensional wares in the form of sculptural objects declined.

## Studio Pottery

The Industrial Revolution had caused the decline of many of the smaller pottery workshops in England. However, it had also produced a wealthy middle class who could afford to buy craftware. With the advent of the Arts and Crafts movement, the field of studio pottery came to the fore. This new movement with all its aesthetic ideals was based on the premise that all handmade objects should be produced with respect and understanding for the materials used. Above all, items should give pleasure both in the making and in use. These artists and craftsmen believed that society should be offered more than just the soulless mass-produced products of the recent years.

Life size terracotta woman by Jules Dalou, 1883–1902.
*Courtesy of the Trustees of the Tate Gallery*

These smaller studio units gained in popularity. Their products were influenced by the Art Nouveau style that flourished in France. This in its turn had been influenced by Japanese art which had had such an impact on the Impressionists. This fashion in form and decoration travelled across the Atlantic where it was

'Adam and Eve' by Mark Tomlinson, 19″ × 15″ × 6″.

taken up by artist potters such as William Grueby and Louis Comfort Tiffany. They too were followers of the William Morris Arts and Crafts ideals and produced works that relied on low relief shapes of vegetable, plant and animal motifs.

In Britain, studio pottery as a movement took its lead from Bernard Leach. He held many of the Arts and Crafts movement's ideals as well as those of the Japanese with whom he had lived and studied as a young man. He opened his workshop in St Ives in Cornwall in the 1920s and founded a new school of craftsmen who under his teaching and philosophy began to open up studios of their own. A contemporary of Leach, William Staite Murray, held diametrically opposed views in that he felt that ceramics were an art form and should receive that status and be shown in the rarefied atmosphere of galleries and museums. Between these two men and their influences on other artists and craftsmen, there grew up a new awareness of individual approaches. Galleries began showing their works more and more and the makers were perceived in a new light. No longer were they humble artisans but designers and artists in their own right.

Lucie Rie, upon arriving in England from Vienna in 1938, quickly established a reputation for her fine and subtle handling of clay. Her works, though not large, have a grandeur and serene quality. She in turn had a direct influence on one of Britain's most important artist potters, Hans Coper, who worked with her for 10 years. He searched for simplicity and purity of form. He always thought of himself as a potter first and foremost and indeed most of the work he made were vessels but the constant refinement, reworking and sensitive balance that he achieved in his pieces gave them a monumental quality.

Throughout the 1950s and 1960s form and function were beginning to be challenged by modern potters. They were led by the American West Coast artist potters who were experimenting with very avant-garde work. Funk pottery and individual approaches were now the order of the day, and this had a far reaching effect on many artists in Britain. The work produced was highly colourful, executed with great craftsmanship and totally idiosyncratic. In the search for self expression, different methods of construc-

tion, slip casting, handbuilding and throwing, were often combined in one piece. Vivid colours were also introduced which were far removed from the subtle tones favoured by those who had followed the Leach school and the fashions of the time. These three-dimensional objects represented things in a literal sense; others used the juxtaposition of popular visual symbols and abstract forms to challenge many preconceived ideas about the way things should look. This was in tune with artists working in other media and gave the works considerable status in the new gallery situation where they were shown. Unfortunately, these new freedoms also led some people to produce third rate work. The results were unique only in that they sprang from tortured clay and 'appeared' to be 'new' and avant-garde. Added to this is the problem that in our often less than critical hierarchical society, if something appears to fit into whatever is fashionable, then it is found acceptable whether it is good or not.

In Britain and the rest of the Western world our position is felicitous in that we are exposed to so many cultural influences. The meso American and European traditional forms and images combined with pop artefacts, graffiti and all the other visual symbols that we are bombarded with in our daily lives have had an influence on the work that artists are producing now. Cultish chic also still has a strong pull and reward. Nowadays since there is little need to make sacred art anymore, we do not work from religious convictions in the same way as those early artists. They, however humble, gave their objects meaning, visual poise and imbued them with an intense feeling of inner spirituality. Many of these, whether used for ritualistic purposes or simple folk forms, have been produced with a clear conviction from the maker and the role and purpose they were to perform in the social setting. Hence the power that many of them exude is derived from the psyche itself and not just a slavish gesture to reproduce art as yet another consumer product. Our modern folk forms and the street culture they feed are no longer produced from this clear conviction of the role they are to play in modern society. It is a dilemma that all art is caught up in. As with all those archetypal figures created to embody nourishment and the glorification of some deity made so long ago by a forgotten hand, the fun-

damental need is still with us to continue to create things of beauty and to extend our creative horizons however tenuous this might seem in these uncertain times. One of ceramics' contemporary roles is surely that it continues to provide a domestic scale giving us as individuals an opportunity for aesthetic consolation and enrichment in our daily lives.

Pot by Hans Coper, height 54cm. Stoneware, 1968.
*Courtesy of the Trustees of the Victoria and Albert Museum.*

*16*

# Gallery

Tall blue vessel by Alison Britton, earthenware, 1984.
*Cleveland County Museums Service.*

Above
'Red leaning Man' by Christie Brown, 24″ × 24″ × 5″.
Slab built and modelled, fired to 1160°C.


Left
Full sized figure by Mo Jupp.
Reduced stoneware.


Right
'Plant', handbuilt form by Richard Slee.
Photograph by Stephen Brayne.

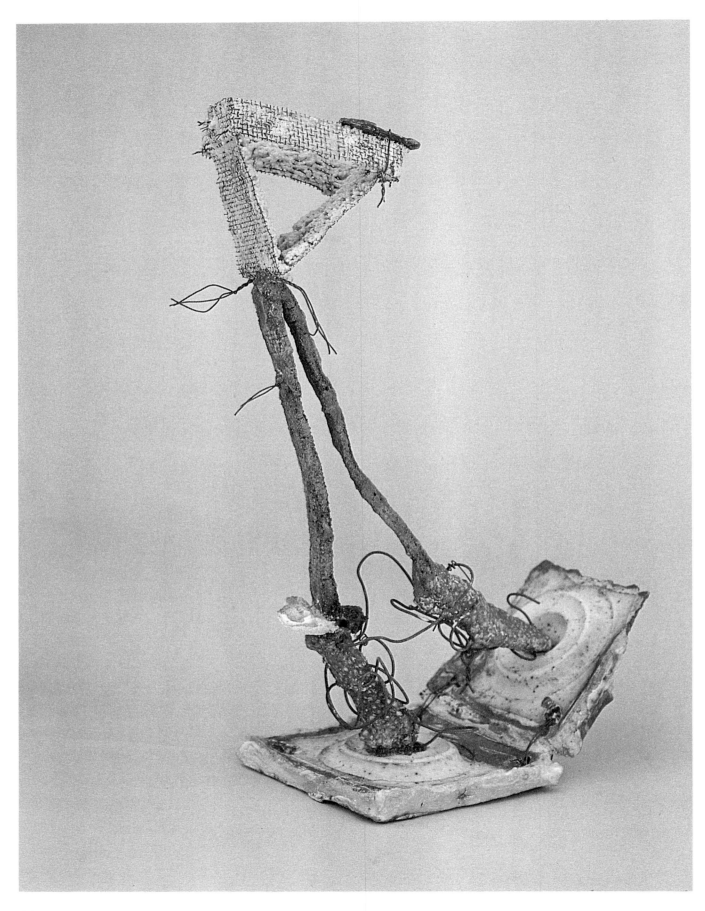

Left
Form by Gillian Lowndes.
The sections are made separately and assembled after firing. The top sections are built in stainless steel mesh with Egyptian paste pressed through and painted with vanadium pentoxide and underglaze colours. Nichrome wire is pressed through the clay section. The tiles are freely cast in white and copper earthenware slips glazed with a lithium glaze and fired to 1040°C.

Right
'Venus et Amour' by Philip Eglin.
Earthenware, slabbed and coiled.

Below
Form by Gordon Baldwin.
Slabbed and handbuilt form, monochromatic decoration.
Photographed by Stephen Brayne.

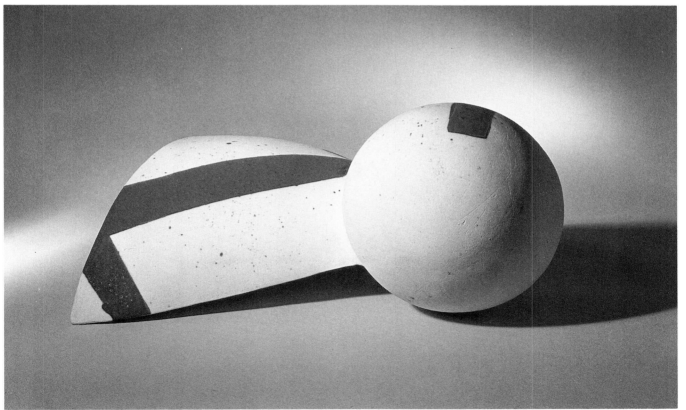

Above
'Two volumes' by David Scott.
Thrown, altered, extruded handle, reactive slip under
earthenware glaze.

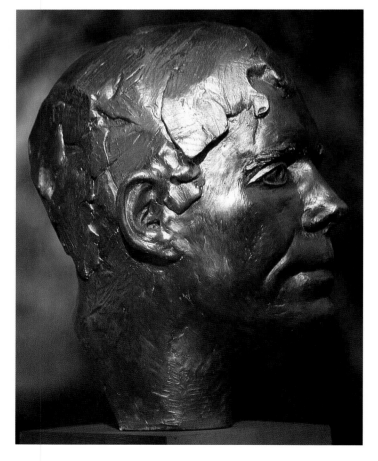

Right
Portrait head by the Author.
Stoneware. Matt glaze, zebrite, life size.

Above
Lidded vessel by Jeff Mincham, 1990, 52cm long.
Coil built and carved form, copper matt, raku, reduced.
Photograph by Grant Hancock.

Detail of teapot form by David Miller.
Example of vitreous engobe and stains, raku-fired (950–1000°C), smoked in sawdust and paper.

# Clays, Glazes and Slips

## Clay

There seems to be no need to describe at length the formation of either residual or sedimentary clays. Suffice it to say that, having been created through either hypogene or supergene processes, residual clays are found in the area where they were formed, and sedimentary clays are made up from deposits which may have been carried long distances by moving waters, rivers and oceans before leaching out and being deposited in a new geographic site. The classifications of the four main groups of clay body mixes that are of most use to the ceramicist are:

> Raku body
> Earthenware body
> Stoneware body
> Porcelain body

### Raku – firing range 700–1060°C

The term raku refers to a technique which originated in Japan in the 16th century. In the process, the clay piece is removed from the kiln during the firing when the glaze is molten and either air cooled or plunged into water to create the characteristic crazing of the glaze. It may also be transferred from the kiln to a combustible material (e.g. sawdust) to cause a localised reduction after which it can be fast-cooled by immersion in water to arrest the effects. All of these actions subject the clay to extreme thermal shock. Later on the piece may have various other post-firing techniques applied which may put the piece under further stress. It is therefore important when selecting your clays for raku work that you ensure that they are strong enough to withstand these various treatments. This usually means that you will need a body mix made up of a clay base with additions of grogs, sand, plastic clays or colourants. The

Teapot form by David Miller, height 22 cm.
Thrown and handbuilt with vitreous engobes and stains,
post-smoked in sawdust and paper
**Note**: Post-firing method
A mixture of light and heavy reduction can give a halo
effect around the decorated areas. This is accomplished by
removing the piece from the kiln and placing it on a bed
of sawdust in a metal container. This, combined with
precisely placed pieces of newspaper, will create areas of
more intense reduction in intermittent waves.

additions will vary in accordance with your requirements for the piece.

Raku clays need to be refractory. A crank mixture of coarse, open clay with additions of grog is suitable as is T-material (Treforest) which has a finer particle size. Crank is a very strong material in both its raw and fired states. This is important in raku work because of the thermal shocks inherent in the process. Crank is pink in colour when fired to bisque temperature (850°C), tan at stoneware temperature (1200°C) and a dark brick red colour with heavy iron spots when subjected to reduction. T-material, which is white in colour, is also very strong and resistant to warping. This is due to the Molochite that is included in the mixture. Both of these bodies can be used on their own or mixed with other clays. There are also pre-mixed commercial clays which are specifically made for raku work. All of these clays and mixtures are readily available from pottery suppliers.

Whatever the choice of clay body, the nature of this firing technique at fairly low temperatures means that the resulting work will always be fairly soft and friable, as well as porous in its finished state. As a consequence, a great deal of raku is fragile and not very practical for domestic wares or for pieces which are to remain outside, for they may be damaged by adverse weather conditions.

### Earthenware – firing range 1000–1150°C

Earthenware refers to pottery which is not vitrified when fired but instead remains opaque and porous. The fired body must have a porosity of more than 5% to qualify for the term. Earthenware is often classified according to the firing temperature, glaze application or other qualities. Well-known varieties of earthenware are the faience wares, maiolica and Delftware as well as the great varieties of low-fired British wares such as creamware, slipware, Mocha and lustre wares.

Earthenwares tend to be divided by their colour into either red or white. The red variety has an average firing range of between 1000°C and 1150°C, and the white between 1100°C and 1200°C. Both remain porous when fired and the glaze that is applied to them acts as a coating. It does not combine with the surface as it does

Tilted pot, two spouts by Alison Britton.

with higher firing materials. This can lead to problems if the work is to contain liquids, and careful glaze adjustments must be made to ensure a glaze fit which will compensate for the porosity of the body.

Terracotta is the name given to red earthenwares. The raw clay can be many colours from

soft yellow to red-browns to blue greys. The terracotta clay body has a variable contamination of mineral and vegetable materials in it. It also contains 10–15% iron (and/or boric) oxide which is what gives it its red colour. Earthenwares tend to have a dense smooth texture unless sand or grog has been added to the clay body.

This material has been used for thousands of years all over the world. Many early civilisations from the Mayas in Central America to the Greeks and Romans in Europe employed it as one of their favourite media for making a great variety of domestic and votive wares.

White earthenware clay is lighter burning since it has less iron present in the mixture. It has many of the same properties as the red earthenware clays but the firing range is higher as it is more refractory. It is ideal for staining with oxides and body stains and it provides a clean bright surface for decoration.

Candlestick, 'Cod and Waves and Boat', by Anna Lambert, height 24".
Earthenware.

'Egg press' by Delan Cookson.
Stoneware/porcelain and glass.

Triptych by Eileen Lewenstein, height 8". Modelled porcelain with a turquoise glaze.

### Stoneware – firing range 1200–1300°C

Stoneware clays can come in great variety, ranging from fine throwing bodies to much coarser sculptural marls. They all need to be plastic and have a reasonable workable strength. Most of them vitrify at high temperature and fuse with the glaze coating creating a strong and impervious body. Most stoneware clays can be fired both in oxidation and reduction atmospheres to temperatures up to 1300°C – in some cases higher.

Stoneware bodies are usually made up from natural ball clays with additions of grog, sand or other clays. There are many suitable commercial mixes available. The darker blends can give subdued and subtle body colours in reduction atmospheres. Most of the stoneware bodies can be used in a variety of different techniques.

### Porcelain – firing range 1280–1350°C

When porcelain is high fired, the clay body and the glaze fuse together to make a strong, non-porous surface. The clay has a high-shrinkage rate and fires white in oxidation and blue-grey in reduction. When it has Molochite or another opener added to it, thick sections are opaque. When thin, it has a translucent quality that we often associate with the term porcelain.

Porcelain dates back to the early Chinese Han, Tang, and Sung dynasties (206BC–AD1279). The Korean and Japanese cultures have also made extensive use of porcelain though it wasn't until the 18th century that Western potters used it to any great extent.

## Additives for the Clay

These are materials that can be combined with clays to improve various aspects of their workability, making them more plastic, more able to endure thermal stress or to withstand high temperatures, etc.

### Feldspars and Feldspathoids

These are basic flux materials that melt around 1200°C, and can be found as components of both clays and glaze mixtures. Feldspar can make a glaze highly viscous and resistant to running. It also helps porcelain to retain its shape during firing and bonds the clay particles together in other bodies. Thermal shock, which can occur at the cooling stages, can be minimised by use of a flux such as feldspar. Feldspathoids such as talc and petalite will also help to reduce expansion of the body and they encourage the free silica in the clay and glazes to fuse during the firing process. This will help control volume change at the cristobalite and quartz inversion times. In the case of quartz this happens at 573°C and cristobalite at 226°C, bringing about a sudden expansion of the body during heating and contraction on cooling. Spodumene can also be added to help reduce this thermal expansion if used in additions of up to 15%.

### Silica

Quartz or flint (which contain a high amount of silica) can be used in combination with other materials to prevent cracking and give the body a hard-fired strength. Additions must not exceed more than 25% or there is the danger of the body becoming unstable and liable to thermal stress. Both quartz and flint are usually added at around an 80s mesh size, and care must be taken that any iron in the clay does not react as an additional flux in a reduction stoneware mixture. Their lack of impurities is useful when preparing a white body but, as with the addition of sand, a careful watch must be maintained to keep the right balance of silica present in a particular mix.

### Bentonite

This makes for good plasticity but it has a high shrinkage rate due to its fine particle size. However, it must only be added in small quantities or its high silica content may cause problems such

Square grey teapot by John Neely, height 9". Stoneware with granite, reduction fired.

as shattering. This type of plasticiser, like macaloid, added in quantities around 1–3%, helps if the chosen clay mix is short. It should be added to the plastic clay mix in the damp state. If it is added initially to a dry mix, a little vinegar should be included with the water to help in the souring process. This will speed the maturing and ageing of the clay.

### Ball clays

These are ideal clays for use at all temperatures since they are light in colour, have few impurities and are very plastic. This plasticity comes from their fine particle size. However, this in turn means that they are subject to a very high shrinkage rate and are therefore impractical for use on their own. They also contain some fluxes which help them fire to a dense hard body, and with the small amounts of iron present they are ideal for the formulation of stoneware clays when combined with other materials.

### China clay

China clay is found in residual deposits in specific areas of Britain and America. It is formed by the process of kaolinization, that is the decomposition of igneous and metamorphic rocks into a new material. China clay has a large particle size which makes it not very plastic though it is highly refractory. These properties make it invaluable in the preparation of white-firing bodies, adding strength and reducing shrinkage.

### Refractory materials

There are many materials that can be used to open clay bodies or give them greater strength both in their raw state and after firing. Others can be added for their decorative qualities to give texture and tooth to mixtures of smooth, more refined, clays. Sands of differing types can be used as well. The main property of sand as an additive to a body recipe is that it acts as an opening agent, giving the clay greater strength.

Other materials can be added to extend or change the nature of a clay mixture, giving it either rich textures or other desired qualities. Ground-up, pre-fired shards or refractory bricks can be added, and some of these can be stained with oxides before they are combined. In some cases they can be used as a surface decoration only, rubbed or rolled into the clay. Organic materials are often combined in this manner. Lentils and rice can be used to produce rich patterns when added to the clay and then fired out, leaving gaps in the surface. Many other materials may be experimented with for their possible decorative qualities – crushed glass, shells, mica, rusty iron, heavy oxide particles, ground cement, and so on. There are, of course, the following more conventional additives, and all of these can be combined in the body mix to give a particular quality.

Handbuilt organic forms by Alan Wallwork.
Vegetable materials have been rubbed into the surface and fired out to leave texture and patterns. Stoneware, gas fired.

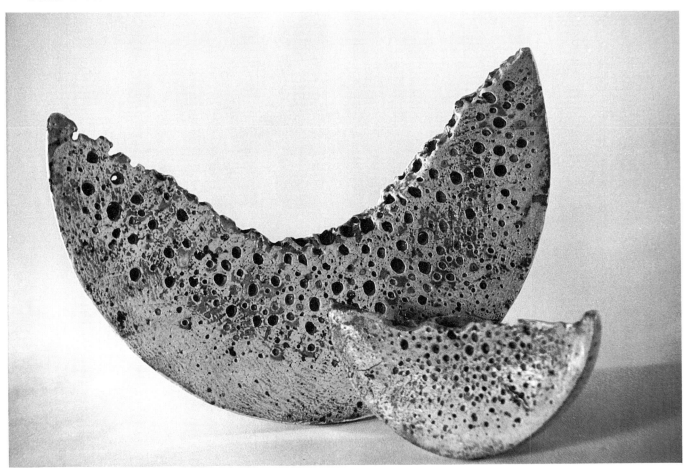

### Grog

This is made from crushed refractory fireclay, pre-shrunk by firing to 1300°C and thereby made inert. It can add greatly to the overall strength of a body mix. It is produced in a number of grades from dust to very coarse sizes that will pass through a 10 mesh sieve.

### Molochite

This is calcined China clay fired to 1500°C. It comes from the manufacturer in a variety of meshed sizes. It is highly refractory and free from impurities, so it is mainly used to open the lighter-burning clay bodies, especially porcelain.

The addition of grog and/or Molochite allows the water in the clay body to evaporate more readily through the porous surface of the clay and it prevents uneven drying and other problems such as warping and cracking during the firing process.

### Fibre

Fibre can be combined with a clay body to give it considerable extra strength in the unfired state. For instance, chopped strand fibres of nylon can be added up to 5%, and although this quantity drastically reduces plasticity, it does have the advantage of reducing shrinkage in the stages of wet to dry. The combination of grogs and fibres works well to strengthen clay pieces and is usually reserved for large sculptural items.

## Clay Preparation Methods

### The slop method

This is a technique where the clay and other materials are combined together in water and mixed thoroughly, either by hand or, in the case of large quantities, using a blunger. The resulting thick slip is then poured into shallow plaster troughs to settle out and dry. Having reached the necessary plastic state the clay can be kneaded and wedged and set aside wrapped in polythene to sour. The longer it is left to mature, the more plastic it will become.

### Dry mixing

As the name implies, this method is done with the ingredients dry in the initial stages. The materials are combined and blended. Then water is added a little at a time until the clay has reached the correct consistency. It should then be wrapped in polythene and set aside to mature. This method does not encourage plasticity so the clay should be left for long periods to sour. When it has reached the required plasticity, prepare it by hand or run it through a pugmill to get it into good condition, i.e. improve its strength and workability for use either for handbuilding or throwing. There are various mechanical aids that can be used if large quantities are to be prepared: blungers and dough mixers greatly help with the physical effort involved and remove some of the tedium from the work.

### Additions of coarse materials

Should you want to include large amounts of heavy or coarse materials to the mix, it is always easier to combine them at the plastic stage because they have a tendency to settle to the bottom when mixing by the previously mentioned methods. To add materials, cut the clay into slices and sprinkle each slice with a layer of the additives and then build up the slices into a stack. Then cut the stack again, this time in the other direction, into manageable lumps, and thoroughly knead and wedge the lumps until the materials are evenly distributed throughout.

## Testing Clay Bodies

Having decided on the particular qualities wanted from a clay, it is always worth making tests to discover its plasticity and the amount of shrinkage that will take place during the firing process.

### Plasticity test

Having made a thorough mixture of all the chosen ingredients using one of the methods described earlier, knead and wedge the clay to prepare it for use. When this has been done, form a test piece by rolling out a small quantity of clay in the shape of a narrow coil on a clean surface. Then bend this coil into a ring. The smaller and more acute the ring that can be made before cracks appear in the surface, the more plastic the clay is. Clearly, if the clay cracks only on a shallow curve then the clay will be short. The plasticity can be altered by the addition of extra ingredients to the recipe.

### Shrinkage test

To make a shrinkage test, roll out a length of the clay to make a bar 13 cm (5″) long, 5 mm (³⁄₈″) thick and 4 cm (1½″) wide. Make two marks on the strip, 10 centimetres apart. The two marks will represent 100 units. Allow the test bar to dry. Then fire it to bisque temperature. Apply a glaze and fire it again to its optimum temperature. Once cooled, the bar can be measured to discover the amount of shrinkage that has taken place. To do this, measure the distance between the two marks on the bar. If, for instance, the distance between the two marks is only 8 cm, then the length of the bar has been reduced by 2 cm or 20%. Therefore, you will have to expect that anything made with this clay will shrink during firing by that percentage.

**Note**: The platelets that form the basic structure of the plastic clay body are hexagonal in shape and are held together by the additional water in the mixture. When this evaporates the particles are drawn together and replace the space that the moisture had taken up. It follows, therefore, that the finer the platelets or body particles, the greater will be the shrinkage that takes place. Coarse mixtures will always tend to have a lower shrinkage rate but also less plasticity.

## Colour Additives to the Clay Batch

### Addition methods

There are a number of ways of combining colour with a particular batch of clay. The best results are achieved with light-burning bodies. Basic oxides, which can give a subdued palette, can be added in dry weights up to 20%. Underglaze colours which offer a wider range of colours can also be added in dry weights. The method for this is as follows: The colouring materials should first be mixed into a solution with water and then run through a fine sieve to make sure that there are no undissolved particles or lumps. This solution should then be mixed with a slip made from the same clay as the body and sieved again before combining it with the bulk of the materials to be stained using the slop method. The clay can then be wedged ready for use or stored in plastic to sour.

Both oxides and underglaze colours can be wedged into a plastic mix but, when working from dry mixture recipes remember to reduce amounts by 20% to adjust for the water content already present in the clay.

One other point: if the work is large, then it would be better to use the oxides and colouring agents in slips and engobes to coat the surface rather than mixing large quantities of coloured clay which can be very expensive.

### Egyptian paste

Egyptian paste, otherwise misleadingly called Egyptian faience by archaeologists, is perhaps a good example of the combination of materials to produce a clay that has special characteristics and colour. It was used by the ancient Egyptians to produce jewellery and small burial objects. It is a self-glazing body that is mixed in the dry state, blended thoroughly and to which water is added to form a thick dough. It can be formed immediately, or wrapped in plastic to store for later use. Once the material has been made into its final shape it must be left untouched so that the soluble salts can rise to the surface and form a crystal covering which will become the glaze. This is then placed in the kiln with as little handling as possible to ensure that the surface coating is not damaged, and then fired to 880°C. The basic mixture is made up from clay, flux and sodium bicarbonate with additions of colouring oxides. It can be difficult to work on a large scale.

### Green ware

As well as being combined in slips, oxides can be applied to green ware to change the colour or enhance decorative qualities. All can be used in various strengths. They give a wide response to different firing procedures but as they are powdery in nature, they need to be combined with a binding agent of some kind. Tragacanth and sugar syrup are both good for this purpose. If you decide to use the oxide diluted with water, the pattern or design may need to be fixed to prevent smudging when dry. This can be done by using a standard fixative spray like those designed for pastel drawings, or a light spray from an atomiser with gum arabic solution. The lighter-burning clays take the application of oxide painting better than those which have a dark-fired body, but any surface can be treated with a pale slip to improve the colour quality before decoration is applied.

### Specific colours

Greens can be obtained from copper and chrome oxides, blues from cobalt while manganese will give browns and greys – with heavy speckled effects. Blacks can be produced by the combination of iron, manganese and copper, or cobalt. There are many variations that can be tried but it must be remembered that these additions will affect the glazes that are applied over them, especially in the case of cobalt and copper as they are very strong in fluxes. Quantities of 1–5% are the usual additions. More can be used for special effects such as obtaining blacks or other saturated combinations. There are no really hard-and-fast rules, and it is open to the individual to try various combinations and tests to find a mixture that gives the desired effect.

All the metallic oxides and carbonates can be used, the former added when the mixture requires large quantities and the latter, which are finer in particle size, for smaller additions. In the case of soluble forms like copper sulphate, some can be combined with water and used to soak reduction materials. When the red-hot work is placed into this, the combined copper will transfer to the surface of the clay.

Copper carbonate and oxide can also be mixed with a little frit (pre-fired glaze material) to produce a wide range of copper matt colours, especially when reduced heavily, giving some startling results from copper-reds through oranges and green blues. If the work is coated and pre-fired to 1000°C, and then cooled, a blow lamp can be used to heat up local areas, and the changing effects of the oxidation and reduction can be frozen by cooling the areas in question with a wet cloth.

### Glazes

All glazes can be coloured by the addition of the materials mentioned. Some will vary depending on the basic glaze components. Those that have acidic or alkaline bases will alter the colours, as will the firing technique from oxidation to reduction.

A glaze applied over an oxide covering will often pick up the colour and can change in appearance. This can be used to advantage and developed as a decorative technique. Raised areas can be wiped clean of stains in order to highlight sculptural additions. Sharp definitions and variations in the form can be exploited in

this manner. Clear glazes are the best for this purpose, applied in a thin, even coat. If too thick, they can become opaque, especially where they gather in deep indentations, obscuring the design.

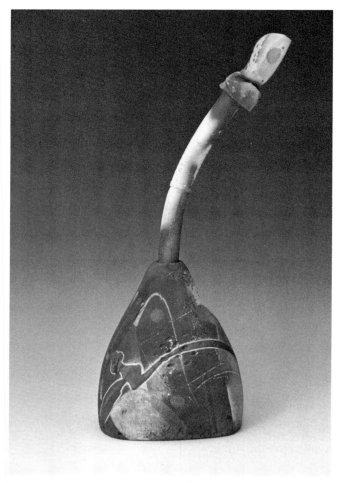

Form by David Miller, height 33 cm.
Thrown and handbuilt, top section rolled and wire cut, vitreous engobe decoration with colour stains. Fired at 950–1000°C and then smoked in sawdust and paper.

## Slips and Engobes

There is very little difference between an engobe and a slip except that an engobe usually refers to an overall coating of the main clay body, made up from a mixture containing 21–51% clay. A slip contains more than 51% clay and can be applied either as a full cover or trailed or brushed onto the surface. Depending on the type of technique in use, slips can be applied to wet or leatherhard surfaces and after the clay has been bisque-fired. The coated surface can be resisted first before the application of various colours, each one used to build up complex patterns as each layer is masked off from the others. If this is done at the leatherhard stage, thin areas can be scratched through to reveal those below, or right through to the original body colour.

Most of the standard decorating techniques can be employed with slips and engobes. Decoration can be painted onto a surface, sprayed through paper stencils, silk screened or trailed in the more traditional methods so widely used in the English earthenware potteries which combined this with combing, marbling and feathering (see p. 83). These methods date back to the earliest times of pottery making, and were employed in many cultures. Slips were developed before glazes as far back as 7,000 years ago in the Middle East and other parts of the world. Even with their limited palette of colours, works of great beauty have survived and can be seen in many collections. It follows that there is a wide variety of uses for slips applied as a decorative medium and these can be developed and adjusted to fit any clay or temperature required. If applied over bisque-fired work, the clay content of the recipe should be adjusted with the addition of calcined China clay and applied in a thin coating to help reduce shrinkage and possible flaking of the surface.

### Slip preparation

White-burning clays can be used as a basis to make up a number of slips. The addition of oxides and stains will create a wide palette of colours. A base mixture is usually made up from clay used in the body, sieved, and added to water until it has reached the required fluid state for dipping or brushing. In the case of low-temperature firings a flux can be added to help bond the slip to the body. Oxides and commercially-made body stains are the best colouring agents and these are added in amounts from small quantities up to 20% depending on the colour required. Larger amounts will tend to cause trouble with the fit of the slip and it can boil and flake during firing. High alkaline glazes can also cause some slips to flake off during the firing so it is always worth testing small quantities before making up large batches.

'Oblique form' by David Scott.
Pinched and modelled earthenware with a glaze over a reactive slip.

## Slip application and treatments

All slips should be mixed thoroughly and passed through an 80s mesh to ensure that there are no lumps and that it has the consistency of a thin cream. If the mix is too thick, it will curtain when dipped and give an uneven coating. If the slip is overloaded with water it will not adhere to the surface but will show the body colour through in a patchy, uneven cover.

Apart from the more obvious additions of colourants, the surface of the clay can be developed in a number of other ways. Slips can be burnished, that is, polished with the back of a spoon or rounded pebble until they have developed a patina or degree of shine on the surface. To do this, care must be taken to catch the clay at the right stage when it is neither too dry or too damp. You must also make sure that it is of a sufficiently small particle size to take this additional treatment. Fine-milled pale-burning ball clays are ideal for this. The use of this method can be seen in the familiar work of the classical Greek and Roman periods. It has a hard, dense slightly waxed-looking surface, red brown and ochre in colour. Those of the Greek period that combined both red brown and black colourants were made up from a fine body mix of terracotta clay. During the firing process, the pottery was heavily reduced and the decorative motifs which were made up from fine fractions of common iron-bearing clays remained black because, in their partially-infused state, they remain unaltered by the effects of reoxidation.

## Terra sigillata

To prepare a basic terra sigillata slip, earthenware clay and water are mixed together into a thin solution. Some deflocculent can be added to help keep the particles in suspension. A specific gravity of 1.2 or less should be aimed for. Milling the clay will also keep the particles small and help them to float. Having prepared the slip, it should be left to settle out and the water decanted off from the mixture. The top third of the remaining slip will be the best for use as terra sigillata. This can then be painted or dipped onto damp or dry ware in a very thin coating. Too thick a covering will cause the slip to crack, for it has a high shrinkage rate. Care and experiment will always pay dividends. Firing temperature is also a factor in producing the desired wax shine effect. Over firing will cause the slip to take on the dry, matt surface of an ordinary engobe. Colour is usually that of the base clay (iron reds from earthenware), but some mixtures can have colour additions or are made from combinations of slips. A simple recipe would be four parts of pale or white ball clay to three parts of an underglaze stain. These can then be polished and fired in an oxidising atmosphere, or smoked to enhance the surface further.

Left
Jug by Angus Suttie

Below
'Wave Box' by Gary Wornell, height 50 cm.
Terra sigillata, slab built.

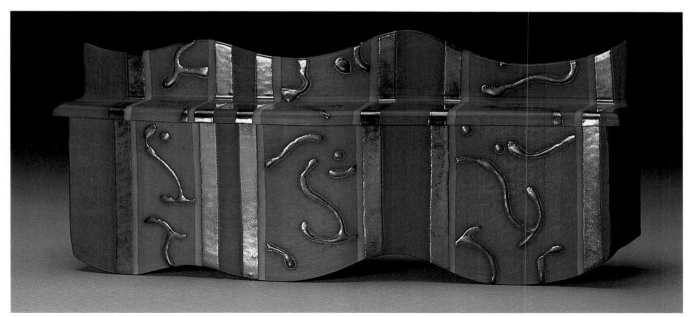

## Colours from oxides and stains

Colour may be added to slips by the use of oxides and colouring agents. Iron oxide in amounts from 2–15% will produce a pale brown colour in oxidation and a dark brown in reduction. It can be used alone as a colourant or in combination with others to modify and adjust their tones. In oxidation atmospheres, either in a clay body or glaze, the material offers a wide range of soft browns to pale tans. In reduction the colours are much stronger in the body mix, and in glazes a radical colour change can take place, giving colours from blue greys through greens to rich blacks.

**Red iron oxide** in amounts from 2–3% gives a tan brown, and in quantities up to 20% will give rich dark browns through to black.

**Cobalt oxide** in amounts from 0.5–5% will give pale blue to dark blue-black colours.

**Cobalt carbonate** in amounts from 1–5% will produce the same colours as the oxide but it comes in a much finer particle size.

Alkaline glazes respond to these two pigments, giving rich, very intense blues. As in the case of most uses of this colouring oxide, it can be softened by the addition of a little iron oxide.

**Vanadium** in amounts from 5–8% will give a yellow to yellow ochre colour.

**Rutile** in amounts from 2–12% will give pink to grey colours and many variations in between depending on what it is combined with and the nature of the firing. It is supplied in both light and dark forms and both contain iron oxide and titanium. It has a tendency to break up colours and give rich mottled effects, flecked blues to gold oranges. It is a good modifier of some of the more harsh colourants.

**Nickel oxide** in amounts from 2–5% will give green through to grey-green colours. When mixed in alkaline glazes it will sometimes give purple to blue colours.

**Manganous oxide** and **manganese dioxide** in amounts from 2–15% will give pale brown to dark brown shades. Purple browns tend to be obtained when this is used in an alkaline glaze, and rich gold-bronze effects at high temperatures.

**Chromium oxide** in amounts from 1–5% will give various green shades and in some base glazes, like those that have tin as an opacifier, pinks can develop, and reds in some lead-based glazes.

**Copper oxide** in amounts from 1–5% will give greens to black. Alkaline-based glazes can react with this oxide to give turquoise and subtle blues, and in reduction anything from pinks to rich oxblood reds. In combination with other materials like dolomite it can produce other variations from blacks to oranges depending on the quantities used.

**Tin oxide** is used as an opacifier in glazes when added in amounts up to 10%, producing a clean white base ideal for decorative work in the style of the maiolica wares of Europe. It can also be used in conjunction with other oxides to form rich coloured glazes.

**Iron chromate** used in amounts from 1–5% gives a light grey colour.

Combinations of some of the above materials will give a further range of colours. For example, try 1% cobalt carbonate, 2% red iron oxide and 0.5% or 1% chromium oxide to produce a turquoise colour; 3% cobalt carbonate, 4% red iron oxide and 3% manganese dioxide will produce a similar colour.

All of these oxides can be tried in combination with one another. They offer a wide ranging palette of colours both for oxidation and reduction firings.

There is, of course, a large array of commercially prepared body and glaze stains offered by manufacturers, and these can be added in quantities of up to 15% or more to white-burning slips and body mixes to extend the range and palette of colours still further.

Left
'Stones and Samson' by Bill McNamara, height 32 cm.
T-material and oxides.

Above
'Prince jug' by Esperanza Romero.
White earthenware body with underglaze decoration, oxidised at 1100°C.

## Underglaze Pigments

This is the method of applying various pigments and oxides in combinations to the bisque ware before a transparent glaze is used to cover the entire surface. The metal oxides that have been mentioned previously, such as iron oxide, copper, cobalt and so on, can be mixed in water and applied to the surface using all the application methods that have been described. There are many commercially produced colours and they cover a wide spectrum, available in pencil, crayon and felt-tips, as well as powdered and pre-mixed forms. All work well at low temperatures, but there is a rather limited amount available that will withstand higher firing.

The powdered forms can be mixed with water and a little glycerine or sugar syrup to extend them and help give a more paint-like quality for smooth application. Additions of gum arabic in the mixture will help the adhesion, or it can be sprayed over the finished decoration to help prevent damage to the design when the glaze is applied. Care must be taken not to let these pigments build up into too thick a layer as this can cause the glaze to blister and lift away from the surface. Various tests should be made to confirm both the correct amount of pigment to be used and their final fired qualities. Low temperature glazes can be used in the same manner as enamels. They will have to be combined with a medium like gum arabic to help them adhere to the surface of the already fired work, which should be pre-warmed to encourage a firm bond between the two. Colours should be applied in several coats, one over the other to ensure an even cover before firing.

Right
Lustred form on a perspex base by Greg Daly, height 16".

## Lustres and Enamels

Lustres and enamels are applied to work that has already been glazed and fired. The work is then refired to the optimum temperature. This causes the lustres and enamels to fuse onto the glazed surface. The secondary firing needed for lustres and enamels is done at low temperatures usually from 700–1000°C depending on the materials used. The range of bright pigments and metallic colours that can be added as decoration in this way is quite large. This is a useful technique because it allows very precise additions and complex patterns to be developed with a great deal of control. This is possible because the medium doesn't run or change form, and it can be applied very much in the way of paints e.g. brush, spraying, air brushing, and silk screen printing methods.

It is believed that the ancient Egyptians were the first to discover and develop the technique. The idea then spread throughout the Islamic world where a variety of fumed colours was used. Eventually it was taken by the Moors to Spain in the 14th and 15th centuries. Meanwhile in the 15th century, the Chinese were also using lustres and enamels as an addition to their underglaze patterns.

The usual method for producing lustres is to fire the wares in oxidation until a dull red heat is reached. Then the kiln is set to reduce heavily until the temperature reaches about 620–720°C when the lustres begin to develop. Fuming can take place at this point when the kiln is just beginning to cool down. Stannous chloride can be introduced into the chamber in small quantities through open ports to react with the glaze surface to give an overall mother-of-pearl iridescence to the work.

Oxidised lustres can be applied and, although they do not always have the same rich qualities of their reduction counterparts, they are predictable in outcome. They depend on the resin that they are mixed with to produce enough carbon to cause a localised reduction to the metal salts, turning them to their bright metallic state.

## Overglaze Colours

Overglaze colours are applied to the powdery glaze surface before the initial firing but must be carefully mixed with turpentine or fat oil for ease of application. They can be thinned further if required for spraying, but must be built up in several coats to prevent possible blistering. This can happen if they are applied too thickly. The usual means of application is a brush, but all methods such as wax resist, sponging, printing and so on, can be experimented with. The decoration should be applied as soon as possible when the glaze coat is still damp or there will be a tendency for the wet pigment to rupture the glaze surface as it takes up the extra moisture. Some glazes are obviously better than others for this means of decoration and the harder the coating when dry the better. If the glaze has a soft powdery surface then it may be necessary to apply some form of binding agent. Gum arabic can be sprayed over it for this purpose, or there are other commercially produced media based on acrylics that can be used as well.

## Glazes and Colouring Agents

There are a number of very good books available that give very specific details of glazes for all firing temperatures and conditions, some of which are listed in the appendix. However, there are applications and techniques that I will mention in general as a starting point for further experimentation.

The state, colour, texture and surface of any glaze is governed strictly by the firing temperature and, with some methods, the kiln atmosphere and post-firing techniques. Glazes are predominantly made up from silica with additions of other materials that cause them to melt at the required temperature. For the sake of simplicity, these various types of glazes can be broken down and described under their temperature values.

### Raku glazes

Raku glazes are subjected to extreme thermal shock when removed from the kiln in their molten state. They are left to air cool, or they are plunged into water after the reduction period. Most begin to flux at around 800° C to 1000°C and fall into two basic categories: acidic (lead frit based glazes) and high alkaline frit glazes. Both

Untitled form by David Suckling, height 105 cm.
Earthenware glazes, slips and engobes.

40

will give clean, bright colours in oxidation but, in reduction, some will change. Copper, for example, will turn from turquoise in oxidation to red in reduction.

There are other ways that this particular firing technique can be experimented with and the boundaries of low-fired glaze applications have been extended into higher temperatures using a mixture of varying glazes. Other ways of affecting the surface are also being developed, for example, introducing salt during the firing, adding materials to the reduction medium, and many others. No longer are the works restricted to the size that can be handled with tongs for removal from the kiln, because ceramic fibres make it possible to construct very light kiln frameworks which can easily be lifted away from the floor of the chamber leaving the fired object in position. There is an endless number of variations within the range of this low-temperature technique, and of the glazes that can be used in conjunction with one another. I have listed on p. 152 a few basic recipes as a starting point for further development.

### Earthenware glazes

Glazes that reach maturity at temperatures between 1000°C and 1150°C are usually considered to be earthenware or mid-temperature glazes. They fall into two basic categories: alkaline and lead-based recipes. Low-temperature alkaline glazes are often very bright and glassy with a tendency to craze and over-fire if not controlled carefully. Lead glazes, on the other hand, have a wider firing range. Most colouring agents give rich smooth surfaces of bright controllable colour. It should be pointed out that most lead glazes that are sold commercially are made from a safe fritted version of the old-fashioned recipes which prescribed the material in its highly poisonous forms. Frits have been referred to before and are produced by heating the flux combined with silica until both melt. The mixture is then introduced to cold water which causes them to shatter. The resulting material is then ground into a fine powder to be used as a safe alternative to the materials in their raw state.

Obviously, some raw materials are poisonous and, if they are to be used, great care must be taken not to inhale or ingest them. Some low-temperature glazes may release toxins after they

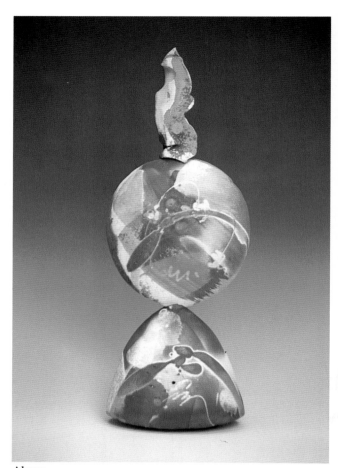

Above
Figure by David Miller, height 40 cm.
Thrown and assembled in three parts, Vitreous engobe decoration with coloured stains. Fired to 950–1000°C and post-smoked in sawdust and paper.

Right
Stoneware vessel by Peter Beard, height 24 cm.
Yellow and pink high temperature glaze stains in final glaze layer. Cone 9 oxidation. Wax resist decoration.

have been fired, especially when combined with copper or when glazed pots are used to contain acidic juices.

Clays that are fired to these mid-temperatures are rarely if ever vitrified. They tend to remain porous unless fired to their maximum. This is the normal procedure, and the glazes that are applied are fired lower to fit and help seal the body.

The range of glazes available for use at this temperature provides the opportunity to develop surface textures with matt or shiny surfaces ranging from those that are just above 1000°C to near vitrified temperatures of 1150°C and higher.

Some basic recipes can be found at the back of the book.

### High temperature glazes

It was probably the Chinese potters who first developed high fired glazes in their huge climbing kilns that were able to reach the required temperatures. Wood ash deposits were probably the first key to possible glaze surfaces along with low-firing clays that melted at stoneware temperatures, as well as some feldspathic rocks. There is such a wealth of resource material and information available on this that there is no need to go into the matter in great detail here. There are, however, two main categories that these glazes fall into and they are those that are fired in oxidation and those that are fired in reduction.

Oxidising glazes are fired in an atmosphere that is clear or neutral such as that in an electric kiln which has no unburnt fuel or gases in the chamber. Reduction, on the other hand, relies on a smokey atmosphere at certain stages of the firing to starve both the clay and glaze of oxygen.

As suggested before, simple mixtures will form a glaze at temperatures above 1200°C and from this very basic principle a wealth of glazes has been developed. Obviously some are more complex and may contain up to six or more ingredients carefully balanced within the recipe.

It is not only the colour in a glaze which is of interest at any of these temperatures; there is also a very wide variety of surface textures that can be used to enhance the work. For example, dry, matt glazes are often used to great effect on sculptural pieces or in combination with other decorative media like vitreous engobes, which are made up from high-clay recipes.

For instance, salt glazing can be carried out at stoneware temperatures and offers yet another option for surface texture. This method of introducing salt into the chamber at around 1220°C causes a chemical change. The sodium from the salt reacts with the silica and other materials present in the clay body to form a glass-like covering with a pronounced orange-peel effect. This surface can be developed further by the addition of slips and other glazes in combination with one another.

I have listed on p. 153 a few basic glaze recipes for firing at high temperatures as a starting point for further investigation.

Right
'Wave rim pike & minnows' by Anna Lambert, 22″ × 14″.
Coiled platter.

# Construction Methods and Decorative Techniques

There are many different methods that can be used when handbuilding ceramics. These range from the ancient methods of coiling and pinching to the use of slabbing, modelling and casting or a combination of these methods. There is also a wide range of decorative techniques that can be employed during the making process, allowing great scope to develop surfaces and forms in conjunction with one another while working on a piece.

## Coiling

This method of making must be one of the oldest methods known to mankind for forming either ceremonial objects or vessels to contain materials for everyday use. Every culture has produced coiled wares from small votive objects to the giant Iberian Tinajas large enough to store 9,000 litres of wine or quantities of grain.

The basic technique is to roll out clay into a series of long sausages on a clean slightly absorbent surface. Roll from the centre out to each end and continue to spread the clay into even coils of the chosen diameter. These can then be cut into the required lengths ready for use. If the coil becomes flattened whilst rolling, apply less pressure and roll the clay over and over on the work surface. Soft clay is often easier to use in this method and will stiffen on the absorbent surface as the coil takes form. Once a quantity of coils has been produced, set them aside on plastic ready for use.

Form a base from clay of the same consistency as that used for the preparation of the coils and begin by adding the first coil, making sure it is firmly attached by pinching and smoothing the two areas of clay together moving some from each coil up and down to form a firm bonding of the two sections. Continue in this manner adding one coil to the other and building up

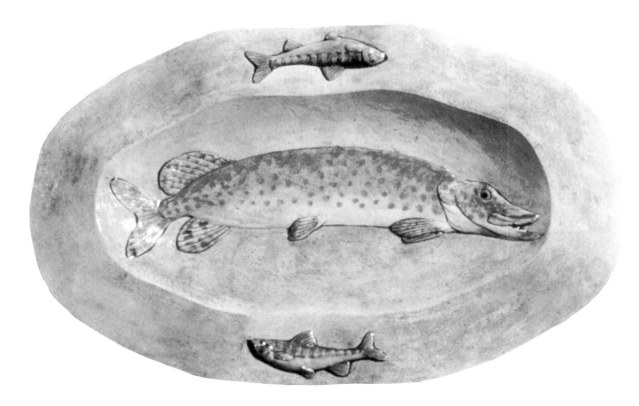

Left
Coiled jar from Thailand.
Incised with a slip decoration.
Photograph by Tony Deane.

Right
Vessel form by Monica Young.
Coil built stoneware.

Below
Coil built figurative vessel
by Sarah Scampton.
Photograph by Stephen Brayne.

towards the final shape. Always try to keep the top leading edge even as the work progresses and never add too much clay at one time in an attempt to speed the progress as this will undoubtedly cause the lower coils to deform and lose their shape, distort or collapse. Once a section has reached the point where it can no longer support its own weight, wrap the top edge with polythene and set it aside to firm up before any more additions are made. A series of coiled forms can be worked on at one time in this manner moving from one to the other to allow each section to dry sufficiently for the next part of the process. Profiles cut from heavy card or hardboard (masonite) are a great help in making sure that the external shape follows the design required. Any irregularity can be paddled out with a wooden bat on the outside, whilst the inner surface is supported. This technique helps to compress the clay walls and ensure that the coils are joined together in a homogeneous mass. Indentations can be treated in the same way from the inside. Gently tap out the clay walls in order to fill out the required shape. Once the basic form has been completed and allowed to dry to the leatherhard stage, the outer surface can be refined using a toothed modelling tool or hacksaw blade to scrape off any unwanted clay. Small indentations can be filled at this stage and surface textures applied.

The construction of any item using this method can, of course, involve the addition of prepared slabs, coils and sections of clay added to one another as long as they are of the same consistency. Large pellets of clay can be used to build up areas quickly and freely. Work in any way that seems to fit with the production of the form in mind as long as the basic rules are observed and the additions of any clay are bonded together in the manner described. Radical changes in direction from, say, horizontal to vertical or *vice versa* will have to be supported with clay buttresses or cardboard until they are able to support themselves, but always take care that too much shrinkage does not take place before these supports are removed. Keep the work covered with a damp cloth and plastic between sessions.

Large thick slabs should be grooved in the back to help reduce the weight of the work and aid in speeding up the drying time.

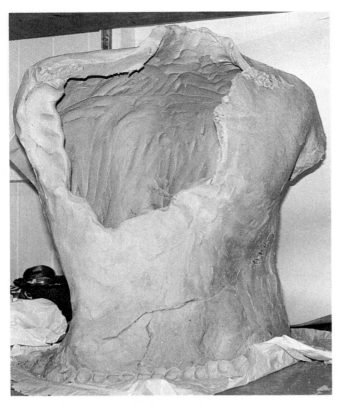

Main section of coil built torso under construction.

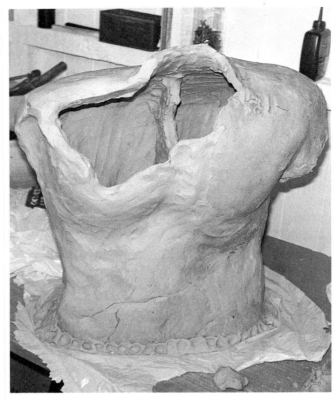

Second stage.

Closing off at neck.

Coil in position to extend neck.

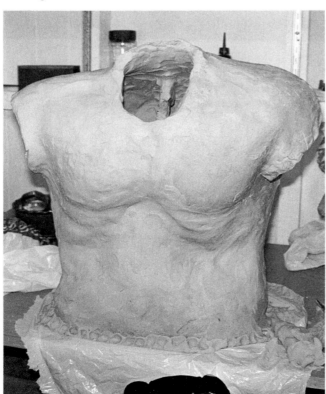

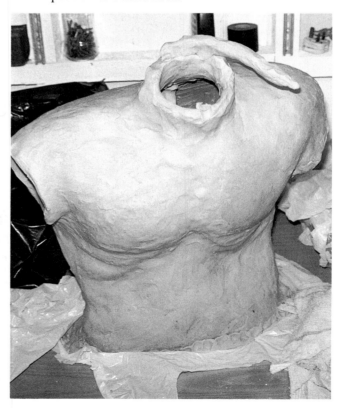

Animal figure by Pamela Mei-Yee Leung.
Coiled and slab construction.

## Slabs

There are a number of methods for making slabs.

### Compressed slabs

When preparing the clay for compressed slabs, remember that large items will require a coarse open clay to remain stable while working. (This will also allow the clay surface to vent moisture during drying.) Delicate items will need a more refined mix with a smaller particle size.

Having prepared the clay, take enough to form the slab size decided on. Knead the clay again, and flatten it out on the bench top to a height of about two inches thick. Then stretch a thin sheet of polythene over a baseboard and place the clay on it between two roller guides. These are simply two pieces of wood cut to the size of the slab to govern its thickness when compressed by the roller. Working steadily, roll the clay until it roughly covers the area of the polythene. Make sure that you work the roller in different directions. This will help prevent warping during the drying process. Keep the roller surface clean, otherwise clay that sticks to it will indent its pattern on to the slab surface. Keep the roller on the two guides and continue until the clay is compacted and covers the area of the slab size.

Larger thick slabs can be rolled out using a cut section of scaffold pole. This adds extra weight, and helps to take some of the effort out of the work. A light sprinkling of grog will help prevent the metal surface of the roller from sticking to the clay.

There are also many mechanical devices on the market for producing clay slabs. Most of them have two rollers that compress the clay on both surfaces. However, they do rely on a hessian (burlap) cloth top and bottom which will give a textured pattern to the surface of the slab. These devices are fully adjustable and can be set at various heights to produce slabs of any thickness and size.

Having produced a slab of the desired thickness, cover it with another sheet of polythene and another board and place the complete sandwich the other way up on the bench. Then remove the first baseboard and polythene and roll again between the roller guides to compact the second surface. This will also help compress the clay sheet evenly on both sides and it will be a further insurance against warping.

The slab can now be moved by picking up the edges of the polythene and set aside for later use. Make sure that the grade of polythene is strong enough to take the weight of the clay lying on it. In the case of very large thick slabs, a sheet of hessian may be a better choice. This method of picking up a sheet of clay can be very useful as it will facilitate placing the slab over a hump mould, or into a former or press mould. Holding the edges of the polythene also prevents distortion of the slab surface and avoids fingerprints and unwanted marks.

### Cast slabs

Thin slabs can be made up from a casting slip produced in the usual manner from pre-mixed clay blended in a blunger to a liquid form and poured into a mould. Almost any casting slip recipe will work for this type of slab production but those with a finer particle size are the more practical choice. Obviously, heavily grogged mixtures would settle out during the casting process and would be impractical for this method of production. For thick slabs and the use of coarse clays, other production methods would be more suitable.

One advantage of casting is that the mould's inner face can have decorative surfaces and complex patterns which will be reproduced on the slabs. As with all slip production methods, there is considerable shrinkage involved and prolonged drying is sometimes required once they have been removed from the plaster case moulds because of the water and deflocculent used. These slabs have a rubbery quality but this does not give them any further ability to follow over curved formers and other contoured surfaces. The advantage of building some pieces from cast slabs is that if complex additions are added they too can be slip cast and will be completely compatible with the rest of the work in progress. This will greatly reduce the problem of sections made from differing techniques cracking or splitting during firing. The one disadvantage is that the slabs must be watched very carefully during the casting and drying period to ensure that they have shrunk free of the mould and that they have solidified in the centre as well as on the outside before they are removed from the plaster. The rubbery quality when first

Rolling slabs on a slab roller with stoneware clay.

Textured cloth laid onto soft slab.

The material is then rolled to impress the pattern into the clay surface.

Porcelain slip is painted over the cloth to produce a pattern through the weave.

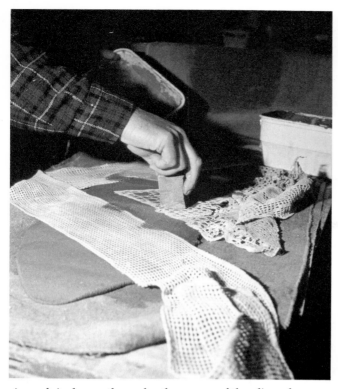

A comb is drawn through other areas of the slipped surface to increase texture and decoration.

Removing the cloth to reveal slip pattern which is slightly raised from the slab surface.

The cut sections are laid out ready for assembly.

The slab sections are laid up into a press mould which supports the clay while the object is constructed.

The construction, having been removed from its supports, is ready for the final slip and glaze decoration. Photographs from Jim Robison.

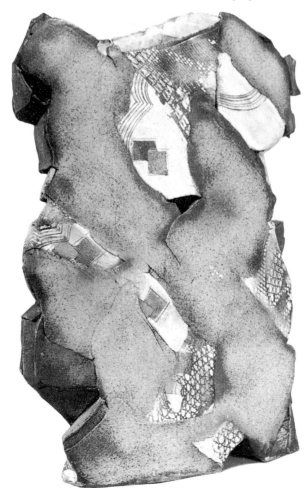

Object by Jim Robison.

removed can soon be rectified by allowing them to stiffen for a short period before assembling. Large numbers of slabs of exactly the same size can be produced in this manner as long as there is enough space available for the moulds, the production of casting slip, and the cast clay slabs in various stages of production.

As with all casting slips, a deflocculent, either soda ash or sodium silicate is used, and tests must be made to find a recipe that works with various clay bodies. Many suppliers will be able to offer a suitable recipe for their own products.

### Drop-out moulds

A simple drop-out mould can be made from wood. This is rather like the old-fashioned method of brick making. A wooden open frame of the size of the slab required is put onto an absorbent board and filled with very soft clay. A wood or steel bar is then dragged over the surface, pressing the mixture into this former. Tamp and push the material until it is firmly compacted over the entire internal space. These slabs can then be set aside to shrink away from the frame which will allow easy removal.

A decorative surface can be cast into a plaster former. The lower face of the mould carries the design and the sides high enough to form the depth of the slab. The leading edges of these plaster sides should be strengthened with strips of wood to prevent too much wear from the bar used to impact and fill the moulds. Once filled, the clay in these frames is left to stiffen in the usual way. Large quantities of ornamental slabs or tiles can be produced in this manner.

### Extrusions

This is the method of pushing clay through a die cut to the chosen design using either attachments to the front of the pugmill or wad-box. Some of the hand-operated extruders can have an expansion box added to the bottom opening, thus enlarging the size of the extrusion into sections of nine to twelve inches. The clay can be passed through the device and produce several sheets of clay at one time or pre-formed shaped squares, rectangles and circles from whatever die is chosen. Coils can also be made in quantity by using dies attached to the opening of a pugmill thereby reducing the aperture for single, thick coils, or making a number of holes for small, narrow ones.

Animal figure by Pamela Mei-Yee Leung. Modelled and decorated earthenware.

### A quick slab making method

Another method for producing a slab quickly is to take a lump of clay that has been roughly flattened out on the bench top, and then throw it in a sideways direction down onto the work area. This stretches the lump out. Repeat the action until the clay has thinned to the required thickness. This method does take some practice, but it can offer some very interesting surfaces especially if the slab has decorative patterns impressed in it. These marks will become stretched and distorted, revealing rich surface textures.

### Cut slabs

Prepare the clay by wedging and kneading, and knock it on the bench into a block with the top face the size of the slabs required. Using a clay harp make the first cut as high as possible to remove any waste and uneven clay from the top of the block. Proceed to work down, cutting slabs of the required size lifting each cut slab and setting them aside to stiffen on an absorbent surface. Check them from time to time, turning them occasionally to prevent uneven drying. Stacks of slabs can be built up with absorbent boards between each layer and left to stiffen to the desired state ready for use. Those at the bottom of the pile must be given the chance to shrink, so it will be necessary to reshuffle the stack from time to time to make sure they are not under undue stress and therefore begin to split or crack. Common sense will tell you when to move the slabs at a stage ready for working.

Do make sure that the stack is not left for too long as the initial drying out will be very fast and it is easy to under-estimate the speed at which this can happen. Once the sheets have reached the stage where they are ready for use, lay them out individually or store them with a sheet of polythene between each layer so that they can cure.

Should you find that the slabs have dried too far, they can be sprayed with water to soften them again or laid on a damp cloth until they have re-absorbed enough water to make them workable.

### Slab construction methods

Once the slabs have dried enough to handle without distorting, they can be cut to shape and assembled. Lay the clay sheet onto a clean flat surface and begin by marking out the shapes lightly with a modelling tool or pencil. When the surface has been scored with the basic outlines of all the sections needed, they can then be cut out using a sharp knife or scalpel and a steel rule. Cardboard templates can be cut and laid onto the clay and moved around to gain the best use of the overall area. This also helps when making items of the same shape and size in large quantities, enabling each section to be marked and cut out in groups. Once all the basic shapes have been prepared they can be assembled into the final design.

Score each edge to be joined and apply a thick coat of slip made up from a mixture of the same clay body as that of the slabs. Slide the two surfaces together, pushing firmly to ensure the two sections are thoroughly bonded by the roughened edges and layer of slip. Wipe any excess slip away from the inside joint, which can be reinforced with a thin coil of clay to strengthen the bonded edges and give a neat finish. This will also help the tension between the two surfaces and decrease the tendency to warp. Where the slabs do not have a decorative surface that can be damaged, a further technique can be used to add even greater strength to the joint: Score the outside edges across from one to the other with deep grooves, and rub a mixture of plastic clay into these. This then acts like a stitch across the two areas of clay. Continue in this manner until the work is completed, and all parts have been joined securely. Always check and re-check that the joints are sealed with slip. Failure to do this may cause a crack to open up during the firing process due to uneven stresses along the seams.

Where possible, try to finish assembling the work in one session especially if it is of a thin and fragile nature. Porcelain, for instance, can become dry very quickly when thin so it may be necessary to lightly spray the work from time to time. However, be careful and do not overdo this or the clay may absorb too much water and start to lose its strength. Large works can be paddled on the joints. This is done by supporting the inside of the joint while the outside surface is beaten firmly with a flat wooden bat. This helps to compact the clay and strengthen the joins. Use a sharp knife and steel ruler to tidy up the edges when the process is completed.

Untitled by Ken Eastman, 40 × 31 × 20 cm.
Slab built, grogged stoneware, painted slip and oxide, fired to 1180°C.

When making objects that have parallel sides, for example a box shape, it often helps to cut a section of slab that bridges across the centre from side to side. This is then left unattached but in position throughout the drying period and can help greatly in preventing the outer walls bowing inward. These supports can be left in place and removed after the bisque firing. Should the form be enclosed, these sections can be attached and left to remain inside for added strength, especially when working on large sculptural forms where the base section might need added support to bear the weight of the clay above. When shapes are less uniform, these bridges may not be practical. The alternative under such circumstances is to use screwed up newspaper or cut foam sponge to help support awkward shapes. This will still allow contraction during drying and aid the clay to retain its original form. This material can be removed when the object is dry or left inside to be fired out later.

### Finishing

Set the completed works aside, lightly wrapped in polythene to ensure that they dry slowly in the initial stages. Once they have become leatherhard, they can be unwrapped and any finishing needed can now be carried out. Large rough areas can be smoothed off using a surform blade on the outside surfaces, and internal areas cleaned of any untidy remains of slip or clay additions left during the making process. If the clay has an open or grogged texture and this is not wanted on the outer surface, a steel kidney worked over the dampened clay will help to push the unwanted particles into the body. Fine, smooth clays can be sponged at this stage to give them the right degree of finish. Once all these processes have been completed and the work on each piece is finished, they should be left to air dry as slowly and evenly as possible. Any forced drying can cause uneven shrinkage of the slabs which, although not apparent before firing, will undoubtedly reveal itself after.

Once the work is dry, the final fettling can be done. A soft scouring pad is ideal for cleaning up any untidy areas. Wire wool is an alternative, but be careful because it does have a tendency to moult small particles that become embedded in the clay surface and, consequently, can react with the glaze in the final firing.

**It is most important that, whenever involved in any activity that causes clay dust, you wear a mask to prevent the inhalation of clay particles.**

'Jane Walking' by Christie Brown, 31" × 5".

### Soft slabs

Clay slabs that have been freshly made by any of the previous methods, rolled or cut, can be used in this following technique. It has a fluid appeal and lends itself to many individual approaches. The basic principle is to use another object to help form the slabs into a variety of different shapes which can then be assembled either in a soft or leatherhard form in the same manner as those in the previous section. A rolling pin is the first obvious choice for a cylindrical vessel.

When using any object as a former, it should be wrapped in some material to prevent the clay from adhering to its surface. Wrap thin paper or cling film around it before laying or wrapping the soft clay over the object in question. Fine muslin is very good for this purpose, especially when the former is of a complex shape, because it allows the clay to take up all the details required. Begin by laying the already covered

Above
Work in progress by Colin Kellam. Stoneware forms built from soft, trimmed slabs.
Photograph by Colin Kellam.

Below
Pot by Colin Kellam, height 32″.
Stoneware piece, having been glazed and fired.

'Legend' by the Author.
Formed from stretched slabs, stoneware fired to 1260°C, porcelain and lustres.

object onto the previously prepared and cut slab, wrap the clay over it, and make any joins necessary before standing the former upright. Prepare a sheet of clay to form the base, luted and scored where the upper section will be attached, and place both sections together and join in the usual manner. This can now be left to stiffen supported where needed by clay of the same consistency or by crumpled paper if the former has been removed. **Never** leave the clay to dry too far while the former is still inside as it will shrink onto the object and render it impossible to separate the two. Do not worry if, when withdrawing the inner section, the paper or cling film remains trapped inside because this will fire out later. Another point worth mentioning when working with soft slabs is always to cut from the outside edge into the centre. This avoids the clay being dragged by the knife blade and distorting the edges.

### Press moulds

The shape of the object should be made up in clay and laid on a flat surface. In the case of a bowl or dish a wooden former can be made and dragged around the basic clay core until a satisfactory finish is achieved. This can be sponged, decorated and finished to achieve the desired final design. A clay wall can then be built around this master and a cast made in the usual manner by pouring plaster into the enclosed area around the object. In the case of a more complex shape, a one- or two-piece mould may be necessary. When the mould has dried, slabs can be laid into the open shape to produce a quantity of work of the same size and proportion. Thin muslin laid inside before the clay is added can help prevent the material from sticking, and aid in lifting the work free from the mould without distortion.

### Hump moulds

Hump moulds are the reverse of those just described. They can be made from plaster or bisque-fired clay. Having formed the inner shape, plaster is poured into this, and in the case of small, simple shapes a stem can be added at the casting stage to form a base projecting out of the plaster. This will allow the hump mould to stand proud of the work top when slabs are laid over it making it easier to trim any waste edges. In the case of bisque moulds, these are modelled directly in clay and fired to 1000°C so they remain slightly absorbent but strong enough to work from.

Press moulded vase by Russell Coates. Porcelain with blue underglaze, enamelled and gilded.

## Body Casting

If you do not have a special plaster room available, always take every precaution to cover all work surfaces with plastic to ensure that no odd pieces of plaster get into the clay at some later time. This can have a disastrous effect when firing.

Good timing and preparation are very important when undertaking this technique and will spare the model a great deal of discomfort. All plastic containers used in the process should be lightly rubbed over with vaseline to help when they are cleaned between mixing sessions and to prevent the build-up of dried plaster adhering to them. Make sure that you have an adequate quantity of water for mixing and cleaning, and also that all tools are near at hand. Prepare the plaster bandage, cutting it into suitable lengths which will make them manageable when dipping and applying them to the surface. Always cut more than you may need. Re-cutting when working on the model is both difficult with plaster on your hands and a waste of time when the cast may be beginning to set. Speed is essential. The bandage can be purchased from specialist suppliers, and is the same as that used in the medical profession to set and protect broken limbs. Any additional plaster should be of fine quality, with a slow setting time.

Prepare the model, having first ensured the removal of all body hair that will be exposed to the wet plaster. If this is not done before casting begins, removal of the cast will be very painful, rather like taking off a giant Bandaid or plaster. Draw onto the model with a felt-tip pen the casting lines at the points where the final two sections of the mould will separate. Make sure that there are no under-cuts and that the two halves will come away from the body without trapping at any point. Once you are satisfied that this has all been done properly, the model should be lightly covered with vaseline or barrier cream. Any areas not being cast can be covered with cling film to protect them.

Place the model in the position required, having made sure that you have chosen a pose which can be maintained, and begin by mixing the plaster. This can be done by eye because a thin solution is needed at this stage. Put a small quantity of water in the mixing bowl and add plaster by the handful until it is heaped in a small island with the top just above the water's surface. This can now be mixed by hand from under the surface. This helps to reduce air bubbles and ensures that all the plaster powder is thoroughly blended. Dip the first section of plaster bandage into the mixture, holding it at each end until it is fully covered with wet plaster and thoroughly dampened, then place it in position on the model. Continue in this manner until the area in question is covered. Creamy plaster can be basted onto the bandage when in position to ensure that the plaster in the bandage scrim is wet enough to take up all the details of the cast. Pay particular care at this stage to the edges where the mould sections meet at the points drawn on the model. These should be built up to about an inch in thickness and smoothed as carefully as possible to ensure that the second section of the cast does not lock onto any rough surface. When the plaster and bandage have been applied to a thickness of about half an inch it can be left to set. This will only take a short time once the chemical action starts and the plaster begins to heat up. Should you think it is necessary, the mould can be reinforced at this stage by strips of wood applied to the outside. These can be attached by using more plaster-covered bandage. Once you are satisfied that the first section is finished, pause and allow the cast to harden before continuing with the next section. Cover all the plaster edges that will come into direct contact with one another with vaseline and prepare all the materials in readiness as before.

Proceed with the second side, covering the area quickly making sure the second set of flanges at the edges are built up in the same way and that they seat together against the first cast with no gaps. Once the second section has been finished, leave the mould in position on the model until it has had time to set. Mark the two sections at various points with a permanent pen to help locate the two halves when putting them together after the mould has been removed. Carefully ease the first section away from the body of the model and check that it has taken the detail required. Then remove the other half. Place the two sections together as soon as you are satisfied that the inner faces of the two moulds are what you want, and tie them together with rope in order to prevent the plaster distorting in the later stages of drying. The entire casting should be then left to air-dry for several days before a rough pressing can be taken.

### Rough pressing

The two halves of the mould will be fairly fragile so treat them with care. The half inch of plaster may also be brittle, and crack if treated to undue stress. Lay one section onto a foam support and begin by filling the mould with a sheet of clay about one inch thick, pressing this firmly down to pick up the contours of the form. Do the same with the second half and leave the clay to stiffen and shrink away from the plaster before the sections are removed from the moulds. There will probably be flakes of plaster and vaseline deposits on this first cast so it is always worth doing this job with waste clay. It will give a working idea of how the final pressings will look, and show up any faults or other problems in the casting. Once the moulds have been cleaned up in this manner, make any repairs necessary with small additions of plaster until the moulds are ready for use. However, note that they will last only for a short time before beginning to break down.

To make a pressing from the two halves of the mould, begin by laying prepared clay into the two halves as described above, ensuring that the clay is pressed firmly into all the spaces and that no gaps are left. Check that the layer of clay is even over all the area of the plaster surface. If not, add more where needed. Once this has been completed, the two sections can then be lined up and tied together in readiness for making the final join. Check that the two halves are in the correct position using the guide marks made on the outer cases of the plaster. Once you are satisfied that everything is lined up, the joins can be filled. Use clay of the same consistency as that used for the pressing, form it into short coils and push these firmly into all the joints until you are satisfied that all gaps are filled. Leave the mould, and allow the clay to become firm enough to support its own weight before any attempt is made to remove the plaster casing. Once this stage has been reached, take great care when easing the first section away. If it shows any sign of sticking and does not release easily, wait a little longer before continuing. Once it is ready, remove the two halves and check that all joins are satisfactory. Make any repairs to the seams or modelling that may need final adjustments. At the leatherhard stage give the work whatever decorative surface you have chosen. Then it can be covered lightly in plastic and left to dry slowly.

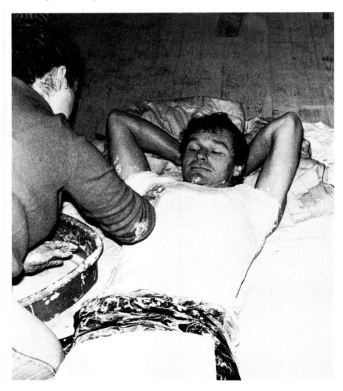

Making a plaster body cast.

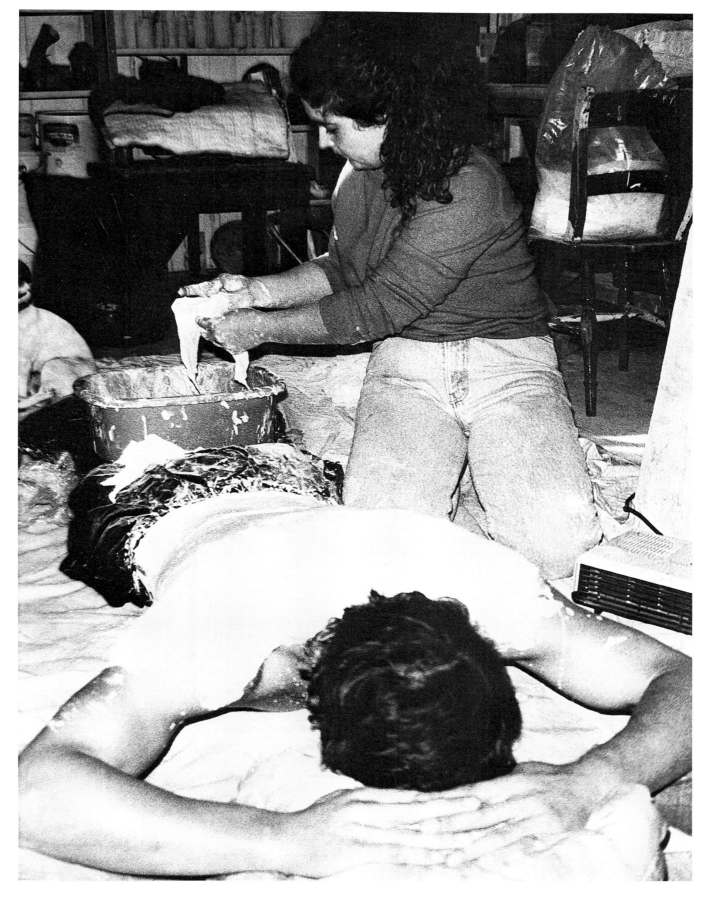

## Modelling on an Armature

This is the most direct method of clay sculpture, and is usually reserved for more complex, one-off items. Portraits, for example, lend themselves to this way of working when only one finished piece is required. The armature is the first important item to prepare. It must be strong enough to support the weight of clay that is going to be added to it, and it is always better to over-estimate this to prevent any problems as the work progresses. Having made a strong base and stem to work from, use armature wire to form the basic shape. In the case of a portrait bust, for example, this must have the proportions of the head in question but made, overall, smaller than the outer measurements of the finished clay surface in order to allow for the later modelling. There will, of course, be the fired shrinkage to make allowances for if the bust is to be life-size and this must be worked out from tests made from whatever mixture or body being used.

Once the armature has been prepared, the bulk of the inside area can be filled with screwed-up newspaper or rags to cut down on the quantity of clay needed for this stage of the work. An old cotton bag filled with sand can also be used for this core section. Tie the bottom end and allow it to remain sticking out of the base so that it can easily be undone. The contents can then run out and the bag be withdrawn through the hole in the base when the work is completed. In some cases, if the armature is made entirely of wood and paper, it can be left inside to be burnt out during the firing. Allowances must be made for the outer clay structure to shrink enough during the drying stages without locking onto the support and causing cracking.

In the case of a solid armature made up of wood and wire, the bust can be modelled to the point of completion and allowed to stiffen enough to be handled without causing too much damage. Once this point is reached, cut through from one side to the other using a sharp knife or wire, and separate the head into two halves at a point just behind the ears from the neck up over the crown and down the other side. Carefully separate the front from the back and remove the armature. Any excess clay can be scraped out at this stage and a final trimming done before the two halves are joined in the usual manner using the scoring and slip method. If possible, try and add clay to the inner seam to ensure a complete bonding of the two edges. Then the final modelling can be completed on the outer surface before drying.

Right
Sculpture of head by the Author, height 2'6".
Reduction fired stoneware.

Life-sized bust by
Helen Ridehalgh.

## Large-scale Works

The materials needed for the production of ceramic forms on a large scale are much the same as those discussed in the previous chapter on the selection of clays. The only difference may be that they might need to have larger particles in the form of openers to scale up to the size of work to be produced. An important consideration is also the amount of compressed weight that the lower parts of the form may have to bear and how thick these walls will have to be to support it.

Most very large works will be situated in the open air when completed and this will create other restrictions in that the fired clay will have to be frost proof. This means that the material will have to be fired to a stage of vitrification or rendered waterproof in some other manner. There are several ways that this can be achieved: one of these is to give the surface several coats of hot wax which is then polished. This does tend to wear off over a period of weathering. A coat of fibreglass resin is far more permanent and can be stained with colours or metal powders if needed. When these materials are used, great care must be taken to ensure that every part of the surface is treated and that no water can enter the clay and cause frost damage later.

A better solution would be to choose a clay for the proposed structure that will be strong enough to remain outside in all weather conditions without any further treatment. This will mean that the body will have to be fully matured during the firing process which can cause difficulties. For instance, there is the added possibility that the stresses involved at high temperatures can cause the walls to crack or deform due to the weight of the object. Another point to remember is that large items will have to be moved into the firing chamber and may have to be lifted or manoeuvred in some manner. This could cause damage to the modelling or other parts of the structure as even thick clay can be susceptible to breakage. A car kiln is one way of overcoming the problem enabling the finished work to be guided into the chamber on rails. An alternative would be to cut the work into sections at the leatherhard stage, then reassemble it after the firing has been completed. However, it would be difficult to design all ceramic structures so that they could be cut in this way and

then reconstructed. Joints may be visible and, in many cases, are hard to disguise causing distraction from the overall feel of the piece. Another alternative is to build the work on a hearth and then construct a kiln around it so that no handling or movement is needed until all the processes are complete. This method is described later on in the chapter on kilns and firing methods.

Once the basic design and choice of materials have been decided upon, construction can begin. The lower parts should be thick enough to bear the weight of those above and any internal buttressing built up as the work progresses. When all is complete, the clay will have to be left to dry and, as in the case of all thick walled pieces, this may take a considerable time, especially as the inside of the work may be enclosed and therefore will not receive the additional benefit of moving air over its surface.

Most studio situations do not allow the space for special drying facilities with the infrared heaters and dehumidifiers that are used in industrial concerns. However, there are some simpler ways to help encourage steady and even drying. When the work is not fully enclosed, a simple electric light bulb can be suspended inside to give off a very gentle heat and also encourage the possible movement of air. The bulbs produced for use by farmers to keep young animals warm give off a greater heat and can be used as a follow up after the domestic bulb has done the initial work.

Another method that I have used when making large-scale works is to build the object up to the halfway stage and then insert a soil heating cable, the type that is placed under the surface of the growing medium in a greenhouse. They come in various lengths and can be threaded around the inside of the structure as the work progresses. Once the item is finished only a very small hole is left where the heating cable protrudes, and the connection can be made to the power supply. Take care when using this method that the initial heat output is not too great and thereby causes cracking. Some types of cable available have thermostatic controls and can be regulated to prevent this problem.

'The Stations of the Cross' mural by Michael Flynn. Raku.

1st Station of the Cross (1989), 24″ × 15″.

64

2nd Station of the Cross (1989), 24″ × 15″.

7th Station of the Cross (1989), height 21″.

12th Station of the Cross (1989), height 24".

13th Station of the Cross (1989), height 23".

Construction of a sculpture by Jim Robison.
The photographs show the basic core construction before
fired clay additions are built over it.

'Goddess of Being' by Sandy Brown, height 3'.
Stoneware with crank body, coloured glazes.

Exterior sculpture by David Vandekop.

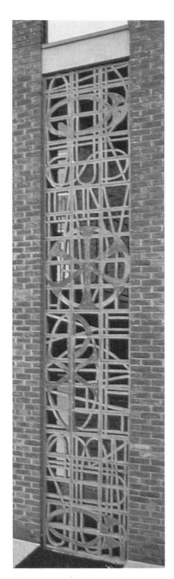

Screen for the Covent of
Our Lady of Sion by Eileen
Lewenstein, height 20'.
Grogged stoneware, painted
with synthetic yellow iron
oxide, thickly applied,
pooling to green/grey –
thin it is Indian red.

Right
Fragments by Michael Flynn 1990.

Once the drying process is underway, consideration should be given to the overall contraction of the clay walls and in particular to the base section. This is probably carrying a great deal of weight and will need to be allowed to contract without snagging on the base on which it stands. Initially this should have a thick layer of sand or grog between the two surfaces, alternatively the work can be built on a thick slab of clay made from the same mix used for the general construction, this will shrink at the same speed as the rest of the clay above.

One further method is to construct the hearth in such a manner that it can contract and move with the general shrinkage taking place above. A layer of pre-fired clay rollers, made in sections about six inches in length and one and a half inches in diameter, should be laid down. They should be placed end to end to form rows the width of the intended hearth, each row in line behind the next, covering the length of the base. On top of these rollers a brick base should be constructed with gaps between the rollers to allow for any movement or contraction that takes place above. The next layer can be made from either a single pad of clay on which to begin the construction or formed from several sections like large tiles that will shrink slowly, avoiding any cracking in this base.

In the case of some large constructions it may also be necessary to support parts of the structure as it is completed, using a scaffolding method made from clay of the same type as the rest of the piece. This can be formed from extruded hollow lengths of either round or square sections placed in position to hold up areas that may not otherwise be able to retain their shape or carry the weight of the structure above. Where these supports touch the clay they can have a small piece of cling film between them to prevent the two surfaces joining, which can happen as the compressed weight settles down and pushes the two clays together.

## Mural Construction

This technique incorporates those that have been described in the previous methods of making handbuilt ceramic objects. There are one or two other basic principles to follow. First and foremost, careful measurement must always be made on the site where the work is finally to be mounted, and a check made that the surface will be strong enough to take the weight at the fixing points where the panels will be attached. Make sure that there are no uneven surfaces to contend with, or things such as lighting cables or water pipes that could interfere with the overall positioning of the finished work. Once these preparations have been made and the design drawn out to scale, work can begin on the construction.

Prepare a clean, flat area to work on. If the scale is very large, a concrete floor is ideal. Check it over to ensure that there are no areas badly pitted or damaged before proceeding. Dust the whole surface with a generous quantity of sand or grog and lay out sheets of newspaper over the entire area. This will allow the mass of clay to shrink and contract easily as it begins to dry, preventing it from sticking at any point. Thin polythene should also be laid out over the paper as an added precaution at this stage before the main work begins.

Having made these preparations, check that the outside measurements are correct for the unfired mural and that all is in readiness to begin the main construction. Begin by covering the area in cut slabs of clay, pounding them down into a homogeneous mass over the entire area to the thickness required for the basic background. Make sure that there are no seams or gaps in this large sheet of clay as it will carry the rest of the design and must be prepared with care to prevent any problems developing later as the work progresses.

Having reached this stage, the scale drawing can be used as a guide to continue with whatever three-dimensional surface is to be built up onto the background from pressed, thrown or directly modelled additions of clay. Try to work across the whole area in stages so that the overall design is maintained at each stage. This is important so that a check can be kept from the design pattern and that no one area is completed too early and, therefore, might be in danger of drying before the rest has been finished. When leaving the work between sessions, spray lightly with water and keep it covered with polythene to maintain the correct dampness of surface to continue with further additions.

When the mural has been finished, it can be left uncovered and allowed to firm up to a stage

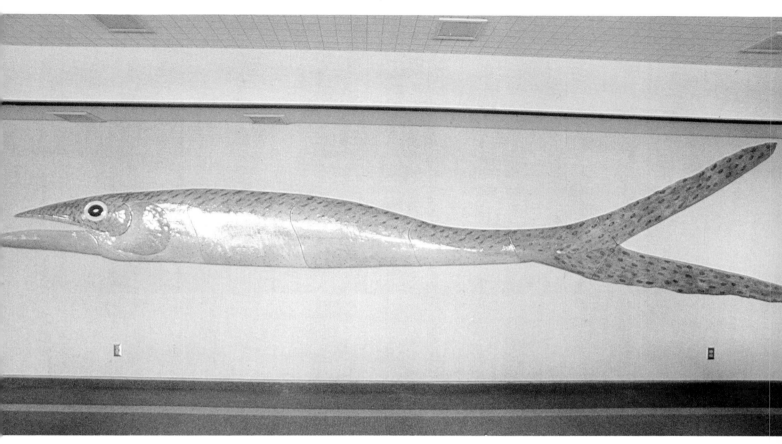

'Montana Fish' mural by Mark Tomlinson, 6' × 24' × 6".

where it will be necessary to begin to cut it into the sections ready to dry and fire. Use a very sharp knife and cut through the surface along the lines that have been planned where each section separates from the other. Ensure that these cuts go through to the backing of paper or polythene and that each one is free of the next before leaving them.

When all this preparatory work has been completed and the panels are ready, they should be checked over and given a final trim, or decorated with slips or any other technique that requires the clay to be leatherhard for the processes involved. Leave the panels under polythene for the initial stages of drying before exposing them to the air to complete the process. Once each section is strong enough to be picked up without distorting, they can be put onto a backing board and left uncovered to dry in the usual manner. It is always worth checking the thickness at this stage and some areas can be hollowed out from the back to ensure even wall thickness and thereby aid in the drying of the entire piece.

## Architectural Works

Almost all such pieces are made by the same techniques as described above, and many are made up from pre-formed sections. That is to say, they are modular and formed in the same way that bricks are from slop moulds and built into the structure in the form of decorative panels, ribs cornices, etc.

There are one or two points worth mentioning in this section that will give a working idea of how to deal with some of the problems that may be encountered. For example, it may be necessary to produce a particular item, or restore a damaged area of a building. The criterion is always to try and stay as near to the original in any restoration, both in colour and, of course, size. This means that the first thing to be done is careful testing of materials to ensure that the final fired product will blend in with those already there. Once this has been worked out, production of the unit can be undertaken.

Above
Stoneware egg by Eileen Lewenstein.
Coiled, fired to 1240°C. Made for the Villeroy & Boche
Sculpture Park in Mettlack, Germany.

Below
'Garden' monument by Sandy Brown, 48″ × 52″.
Stoneware.

Below
'Fragments' by Michael Flynn, height 36″.
Stoneware.

Above
Group of five columns by Eileen Lewenstein, height 1 metre.
Stoneware, fired to 1240°C.

Below
'Altarpiece' monument by Michael Flynn, 4'6" × 7', 20" in diameter.
Stoneware.

## Decorative Surfaces

There are a vast number of ways that soft and leatherhard clay can be impressed and decorated and it is only limited by imagination. Since there is such a diversity and variety of means available I can only suggest a few in these pages and leave the individual to discover the rest by experimentation and research.

### Direct impressions

These can be applied to the surface using individual stamps made out of carved plaster blocks or by the use of found objects, such as screw heads, old plastic toys, pieces of wood, buttons, shells, braided cord – anything that can make a mark in the clay surface and which lends itself to the work in progress. These impressed patterns can be added to by scratched lines, carving, rouletting, and so on.

Another method of transferring a pattern to the clay is to roll the slabs out directly on to a plaster bat that has a design carved into it, thus picking up the image in relief. Plaster can be made up especially for this purpose and carved or cast into very complex patterns. Rubber car mats are also very useful for taking repetitive patterns and come in a great variety of shapes, sizes and textures. There are, of course, many other ways of reproducing surface texture, and an infinite number of variations.

Coil constructions can be built up from additions of clay in the manner described earlier, or the individual coils built into the wall can be left untouched on the surface to create a patterned texture. Another method is to lay the coils into a carved or decorated plaster press mould. The internal surface of these is then smoothed over to make the joins between them. Once this is removed from the plaster, the outer face will carry any impression from the plaster. A combination of clays could be used in this manner to produce patterns of differing colours. Try experimenting with this technique, mixing coils and balls of clay to build up intricate surface textures.

### Paddle surfaces

Paddling the surface with various textured bats made from wood can produce very attractive random patterns. These beaters can also be used to compress other materials into the surface: rope, coarse string, leaves – anything that may produce the desired effect. Such materials can be removed or left embedded in the clay surface and, perhaps, used as a means to resist further applications of slips or oxides as the decorating process continues.

Paper doilies, especially if they are made of thick, embossed paper, can be used to imprint their complex patterns onto the surface either by the process of paddling, or by rolling thin sheets of clay over them. These thin slabs of clay are then slipped on the back and added to the outer clay surface in the same manner as any other sprigging technique. Thin coils of clay can be laid onto a plaster bat in a fairly open pattern like lattice-work or, perhaps, in the form of lettering which can then be rolled and added in the same way.

Much deeper patterns can be obtained by slicing through a clay block using a slightly stretched book binding spring. This is pulled through the clay as if it were a normal cutting wire and can be moved as the cut is made to produce some very unusual but regular patterns. If the other side is cut using a conventional smooth wire, this slice can then be added in the manner described above.

Poured patterns can be made up from slips of various colours piped or trailed onto a plaster surface before they have dried and are still tacky to touch. Gently lay a cover of cling film over the top, rubbing just hard enough to allow the clay to stick to its surface. Leave this for a short period and then check that it is free from the plaster before attempting to lift it attached to the cling film. Then transfer the design to the clay surface which should be pre-dampened ready to receive it.

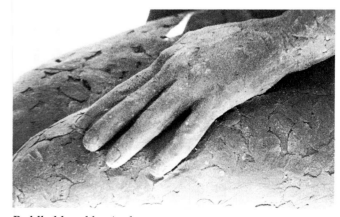

Paddled hand by Author.

## Incising and sgraffito

Incising is a technique of decoration has been used throughout history from early Mesopotamia through to the most avant-garde work of today. It is more often begun at the leatherhard stage and can be achieved with either a sharp wooden tool or metal loop, cutting the pattern or design directly into the surface. Care must be taken that the cuts are not made too deep or cracks may develop if the wall is weakened too much. Stoneware vases of the Tz'u-Chou period in China show this technique at its best where the incised lines are added to by further carving of the clay walls into the most complex and delicate patterns.

Sgraffito is the technique of cutting through one slip surface to another using a variety of tools. This form of incised decoration may be a combination of linear marks and the cutting or scratching away of larger areas. It has its roots buried in the past and examples have been found in Byzantium, Syria and many other parts of the world – China in the Tz'u Chou Sung period, Neolithic pots of the Nile valley, and in early Bronze Age wares.

The work is best done when the clay is at the leatherhard stage and the layer of slip is still soft but not wet. If the surface is too damp, the line will become blurred, or if too dry the edge will be fuzzy and ragged. The tools should be as sharp as possible so that a good clean cut is maintained. A variety of these can be obtained which have recessed spoon blades and rounded or square-sectioned tips. Wire loops are ideal for cutting away larger areas but in general there are no hard and fast rules, and anything that works for the individual is the best approach.

## Combing

Experiment with wooden combs and other objects to see how varied this effect can be. Results will be determined by the size and number of teeth that they have, and how the tool is dragged across the surface.

## Piercing

This technique is carried out by cutting through the outer surface, piercing the wall right through and creating an open lattice pattern. This should be done when the clay is not quite leatherhard

Bowl by Dorothy Feibleman.
Pierced and laminated porcelain.
Photograph by David Cripps.

but cuts cleanly without a ragged edge. Should you wish to develop the technique, various tools can be made from short lengths of thin tubing and used as punches and pattern cutters. The design should be drawn onto the surface before work begins, and all the larger areas of the pattern removed first with a sharp potter's knife. Continue on to the smaller details with any tool that suits the work. Simple hole-cutters can be used to make the initial slice through the wall and then developed into more complex shapes with a scalpel blade. Because of the often fragile nature of the clay lattice left, great care must be taken in the drying process since it differs greatly from the body of the main section of the work. This means that there will be a considerable variation in the shrinkage of the piece, and it will always be worth taking as long as possible over the initial stages of drying in order to prevent cracking the design.

## Fluting

This method of decoration is usually carried out when the clay is soft but just firm enough to be handled. A variety of tools can be used but a simple wire loop works well. This is drawn down the clay, cutting a shallow groove in the surface either in horizontal, diagonal, vertical and spiral patterns.

## Roulettes

These tools are ideal for banding rich patterns onto any clay surface. A very simple tool can be made up by binding string around a short length of dowel. This is then rolled across the surface of the clay under the fingers and palm of the hand to produce a textured pattern. There are, of course, many other materials that can be used in this technique. A short cylinder or stick of plaster that has a pattern carved into its surface can be rolled in the same way. If these roulettes are to be used a great deal, then it will be worth making up a collection that have handles for more convenient use.

To do so, mark or impress a pattern onto a thin slab of clay and then wrap this around to form a small ring with the pattern on the inner face. This is then used as a mould. Pour a small quantity of plaster of Paris into the centre of the ring and, before the plaster sets, insert a plastic drinking straw into the centre to form an axle hole. Having allowed the plaster to set, remove the outer layer of clay, clean up the sides, and cut the waste ends of the straw away. A wire can then be threaded through the central hold and twisted back to form an axle and handle all in one.

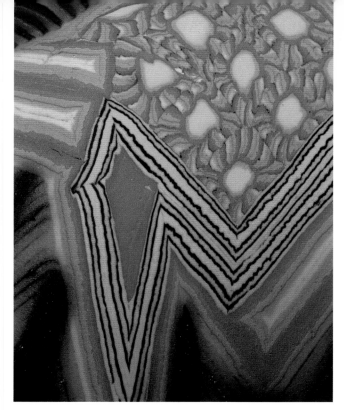

Above
Detail of a piece by Dorothy Feibleman.
Laminated section with over loaded copper.

Below
'Wells Cathedral', slab dish by John Maltby, 9" × 14" wide.
Stoneware with glaze and clay decoration.

## Found objects

There are, of course, an infinite number of objects that can be used to make impressed marks in the surface of soft or leatherhard clay. Printers' typeface can be used not only to impress lettering but also to build up abstract patterns. There are many wonderful Indian wooden textile blocks available in some shops which can be used directly onto the clay surface or used to make rouletting patterns as described above. The list is endless: plastic-textured bags, ropes, wire lattice, wooden mouldings, rubber stamps – you will be able to find many things which can be the starting point of a decorative motif.

Coiled planter from Thailand.
Incised and inlaid slip decoration.
Photograph by Tony Deane.

'Portnoy's complaint no. 1' by Delan Cookson, height 15".
Stoneware/molten glass.

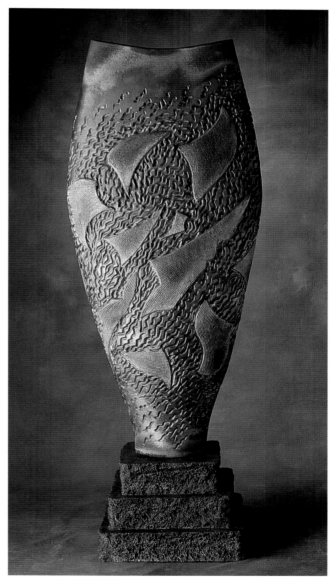

'Fragments of Memory' by Jeff Mincham, height 1.62m.
Post firing, reduced earthenware, 1080°C, with copper matt glazes.

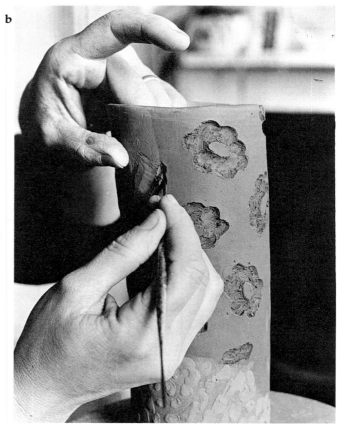

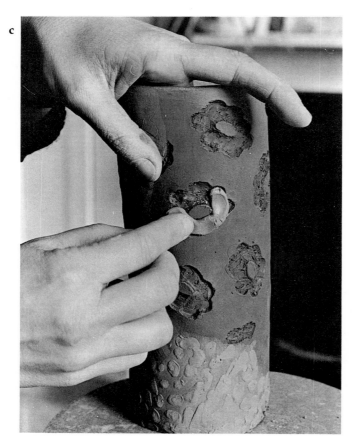

80

## Sprigs

This method of decoration dates back to the early Chinese Han Dynasty and has been used extensively as a decorative medium in the form of friezes, medallions, rosettes and many other embellishments. The sprigs should be applied to the surface when the clay is still soft and attached in position using a slip made up from the same clay. A simple form of sprigging which I have mentioned earlier, is the laying of coils and trailed designs that are then paddled onto the surface. More ornamental sprigs can be pressed or cast in shallow moulds and then added in the same manner, but these have to be handled with great care in order not to damage their decorative surface, and cannot be paddled or pressed. They can be added whilst still in their plaster mould. Score the back lightly and cover in slip. Do the same to the area that is to receive them. Pick up the mould with the sprig still inside and press the two surfaces together firmly. The plaster mould should now pull away, leaving the decorative sprig in position.

Additions of clay in the form of pellets or cut shapes can be attached to the surface in the same manner described above and then, while supporting the inside, various stamps can be pressed into the raised areas to create a relief decoration.

## Inlay

Another technique using the applied method is to carve away the pattern and then rub soft clay of the same body mix into the grooves. This additional clay can be coloured with oxides so that it differs from the main body colour. A pale-burning clay is best for this method since it allows contrasts. Once the additional clay has dried sufficiently, the excess can be scraped away to leave the coloured pattern flush with the surface. If the initial lines are fairly fine, coloured slips can be used in the same way. (This method is known as *mishima* named after the Korean wares imported into Japan around AD 1300.)

Another method is to lay coloured patterns of plastic clay onto the work surface and then roll a slab out over the top, thus forcing the pattern into the body of the slab. Some distortion of the design will take place, but this can be used to advantage. For example, a drier clay can be used for the initial pattern and when the next layer of clay is rolled out over it, small indentations and recessed edges will appear around the joints of the two materials creating further visual effects.

## Agate ware

Agate patterns go right through the clay body. This is achieved by mixing coloured clays

Above
Larger patchwork sheet, ready to be smoothed together with rolling pin. Photograph from Kate Malone.

Left
a. Pinching seam together for a simple cylindrical vase.

b. Carving out a design.

c. Pressing in contrasting colour clay.

d. Scraping off the excess clay.

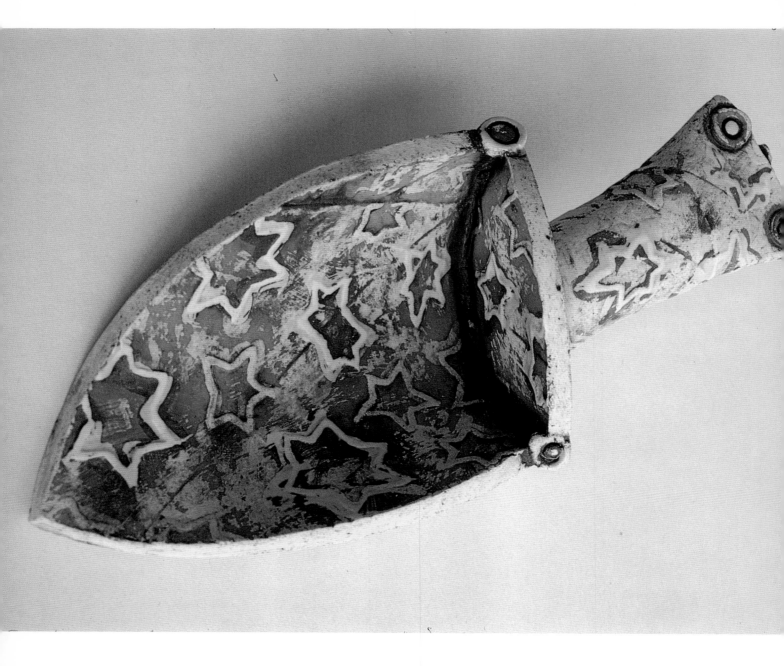

together in their plastic state. The various stained bodies are layered in a sandwich and can be kneaded to produce a swirling pattern in the mixture. The stack of colours can be cut through with a wire, and re-layered many times in a variety of directions to produce rich patterns of lines and shapes.

### Lamination

This technique can be used in a variety of production methods. A design is first of all laid out on a plaster bat. Once the pattern is complete, a sheet of clay is rolled out over the design. This

Spoon by Sharon Blakey, length 8″
Terra sigillata, coloured slips.

compresses and combines the two layers to form a slab that can then be laid into a press mould or cut into sections for assembling into a finished work.

Press moulds can have this sort of design laid directly into them. A backing layer of clay is then applied, and the two combined by gently paddling the inner face of the mould with a pestle covered in muslin. Tests should be carried out to ensure that the combinations of clay are compatible, and will not shrink away from each other as the work dries. Small additions of material, such as Molochite, will help adjust the clay and reduce shrinkage rates in each mixture.

## Marbling

The clay surface is first given a coat of wet, fluid slip. This is then trailed over with another which is of a contrasting colour. Using a broad-toothed comb, the two colours are dragged into a swirled pattern. The slab is then picked up and given a sharp twisting motion that further distorts and swirls the pattern. Once this has been achieved, the slab can be given a sharp tap on the bench in order to flatten out the raised slips.

## Feathering

This technique is very similar to the last. First, the clay is covered with the base slip and the second layer applied through a slip trailer or poured across the surface. A feather or thin lining-brush is then dragged over them, pulling them out, one into the other. This can be left with the raised edges of the slip standing proud or, as in the last case, a sharp tap on the work top will help to flatten and smooth the surface.

## Slip trailing

This process is achieved by piping trailed slip through a rubber bulb with various-sized nozzles, or pouring through a narrow-spouted vessel to produce the same effect. The slip must be prepared very thoroughly and sieved through a 100–120s mesh sieve so that it flows smoothly. The addition of a little sodium silicate will help the fluid quality of the mix, as well as a little gum tragacanth to encourage firm adhesion. Before starting, it is always a good idea to check the flow and texture of the slip on a scrap slab. Try to keep the pressure on the bulb steady so that a free-flowing line is produced. Any hesitation or indecisive movement will leave an unsightly mark. With practice a strong confident line will be produced.

An example of a trailed slip by Svend Bayer.

### Monoprint

This method is much like one described earlier. The slip is trailed onto a plaster surface to produce the decorative pattern but this time, instead of transferring it to another surface, a sheet of clay is laid over it and then rolled between two guides to compress them together. A certain amount of distortion will occur but this is unavoidable. Another variation of this method is to scratch a decorative pattern into a plaster bat, trail slip into the grooves, clean the plaster surface leaving the slip-filled grooves, and then roll the clay out as before to pick up the design in relief.

### Stencilling

This technique, as its name implies, is the method of using positive or negative cut shapes to produce a desired pattern. Newspaper is one of the best materials to use. Having been cut to shape and dampened, it is laid onto the surface of the clay and pressed into position with fingers or a damp sponge. Any paper will do but the softer and more porous the better as long as it does not break down when wet. When the stencil is in position, the slip can be sprayed, brushed or dipped over the area in question. Once this has been done, wait till the shine has gone from the surface and it has begun to dry a little. Check a section by lifting the edge of the paper. If it comes away clean without smudging or leaving a ragged edge, then it is time to remove the entire stencil. This can be done by lifting the corner with a sharp tool or pin, and removing the paper in one smooth action. This process can be continued with layers of other slips and stencils until the design is completed. If required the stencils can remain on the surface between each individual application but care must be taken that the build up of slips is not too thick or that the original paper stencils do not begin to dry out and peel off, causing the slip layers to crack or flake.

### Sponge printing

This is the application of slips or other decorative media transferred directly to the clay surface by the means of a nylon sponge. These commercially-produced synthetic materials come in a variety of textures which can be used to build up rich patterns. Dip the sponge into a thin mixture of slip and, once it is loaded, press it onto the surface of the slab thus transferring a quantity in a thin coat from one to the other.

The dense sponges are ideal for carving into decorative shapes. This can be done by using a sharp craft blade or, if the shape is more complex, a heated wire or knife will serve to burn or carve very complicated patterns into the material. (A mask should always be worn when this is undertaken because the fumes from some of these man-made materials can be very toxic.)

### Brush decoration

As its name implies, this is perhaps one of the simplest ways of applying decoration to a given surface but it can be one of the most versatile and beautiful of all. The subtle and sensitive marks can produce an unending variety of shapes from broad vigorous statements of colour to the most minute detail. The Japanese calligraphic brushes are the most satisfying to use and come in a variety of sizes. They are of course used with great artistry by the Japanese and it would take hour upon hour of practice to even begin to emulate their skills. However, with patience they can be used to create the most beautiful designs and stylised patterns. There are a great number of other brushes that can be experimented with from the humble house painter's brush to the wedge and rigger brushes of the watercolour painter.

### Casting slips

These can be used to advantage as a medium for decoration. The fact that they contain defloculents means that they may need to be tested for shrinkage before adding them to another clay surface in case they contract too much and lose adhesion. In some cases this property can be taken advantage of to produce fascinating, cracked and textural decoration. There are other applications, for example, material such as lace can be soaked in this slip mixture and laid onto another surface. Later, when the piece is fired, the lace or material will burn out leaving only the delicate pattern behind. Try this technique with other materials – cheese cloth or other remnants.

There is another method. Instead of trailing the slip directly onto a slab as described earlier, do the same into a plaster press mould and then fill it with casting slip. Wait till it has taken up the required thickness for a cast and pour away

Vessel by Peter Beard, height 34 cm.
Stoneware, fired to cone 9, oxidation, copper rich top
glaze, slab built, wax resist decoration.

the excess. This, when dried enough, will release and reveal the slip-trailed pattern embedded into the surface of the work.

### Oxides

There are a great many metal oxides that can be
applied to green ware to change the colour or
enhance decorative qualities. Most of these have
been discussed in greater detail in the chapter on
clays, glazes and slips, but there are some applications that work well at this stage of the making
cycle. All can be used in various strengths, and
give a wide response to different firing procedures. As they are powdery in nature they
need to be combined with a binding agent of

some kind – tragacanth or sugar syrup are both
good for this purpose. The pattern or design will
need to be fixed to prevent smudging when dry.
This can be done using a standard fixative spray
like those designed for pastel drawings or a light
spray from an atomizer with gum arabic solution. The lighter-burning clays take the application of oxide painting better than those which
have a dark fired body, but any surface can be
treated with a pale slip to improve the colour
quality before decoration is applied.

# Kilns and Firing

The variations of kiln types are unlimited. Which one is chosen for use is governed by several factors apart from the more obvious one of cost. The first consideration is what temperature the chamber is to reach. Others are the size of the work to be fired, the choice of fuel, the site where the structure is to be built – either inside the studio or outside depending on the available space.

Kilns that are fired with oil or wood will require a chimney of the correct proportions to create the draught needed. Gas kilns will have to be properly vented to the open air if situated inside the studio. Raku kilns will need a large work space around them for manipulation of red hot works removed from the kiln to reduction containers and so on.

Another factor is production quantities; large kilns can contain many items leading to long periods between firings and lengthy firing cycles. This in turn will mean that adequate storage will be needed for green ware and bisque. This can mean a slower production of finished work and perhaps long delays when tests need to be carried out. Chambers that are too small on the other hand can limit the scope of some work and can be uneconomic on fuel costs in relation to each piece that is fired.

In order to clarify these matters a clear idea of exactly what is to be produced should govern the type of kiln chosen. If the work is to be very colourful and rich in graphic decoration, then a low temperature cycle will give greater scope. Mid-temperature firings have nearly the same range of bright colours with the added advantage that the materials are stronger when fired. The higher the temperature rise beyond this point, the more limited the range of colour available but the use of a reduction atmosphere as well as oxidation can offer even more variety to a somewhat restricted palette.

## Updraught kilns

Updraught kilns, as the name implies, rely on the heat from the fuel entering at the bottom of the chamber and passing up and around the wares and escaping out at the top. These simple kiln types have been used for hundreds of years in many cultures. They produce the temperatures at which most earthenware clays are matured. This method was really an extension of the early bonfire or pit firings which used shallow walls to contain the fire. As techniques and firing skills developed, the structures became higher and there was a need to enclose the roof area to control the heat. Initially this was often done by covering the wares in the chamber with broken shards. Later this developed into a more formal arched or domed roof that was part of the permanent structure.

## Downdraught kilns

The basic updraught method of firing was developed in China using a system where the chamber was built on a sloping bank with the fire box at the bottom of the slope and the exit flue at the top. The kiln was basically a form of chimney that was either packed by crawling in through the fire box or through doors constructed in the sides of the chamber.

This method was further developed into the traditional bank or climbing kilns which were made up from a series of separate chambers linked one behind the other, extending up a slope. As before it was fired initially from the bottom, each chamber preheated from the one below as the firing continued. Baffles and bag walls were introduced to deflect heat to various areas and flues were built into the lower back of each chamber.

This slowed down the speed at which the flame passed through each section improving heat retention and creating a more efficient control of the temperature within the chambers. The structure of these kilns meant that the draught was no longer just passing through in the manner of an updraught firing. In fact the passage of

Cross-draught kiln

Fig. 17 *Left*: The up-draught
bottle kiln principle.
    *Above*: The down-draught kiln.
*Right*: The cross-draught kiln.

Bank kiln

fire box

heat changed to a cross draught and then to down draught as the flues, walls and other aspects of the kiln changed in design. Not only did these developments mean that there was greater control of all aspects of the firing process but also much higher temperatures were possible. (See p. 87.)

## Kiln Building Materials

There are many types of brick and other refractories available that can be used for the construction of kilns. Low temperature earthenware and raku kilns can be built using any basic house brick, especially if they have a layer of insulating material as an outer skin. If the temperature requirements are going to be higher, then it will be necessary to build using fire brick. These come in various grades and differing types. The heavy fire brick is dense and hard with little or

no insulating properties which make it ideal for the construction of fire boxes and the base of kiln structures or for specialist methods of firing like salt glazing. The other alternative is high temperature insulating bricks (HTIs) made in an open, porous manner. They are light in weight, strong enough to be used in all areas of kiln construction and have the added quality that they are soft enough to be shaped easily by cutting with a wide toothed saw. Whichever type of brick is chosen, the bricks will have to be backed up with a layer of insulation to help retain the heat. A further insurance against undue heat loss through the walls is to sandwich a layer of tin foil followed by another of ceramic fibre before the outer skin of insulation is built. The metal foil helps to reflect the heat back and the low grade fibre is a very good insulator and in some cases can obviate the need for this last layer of back-up bricks.

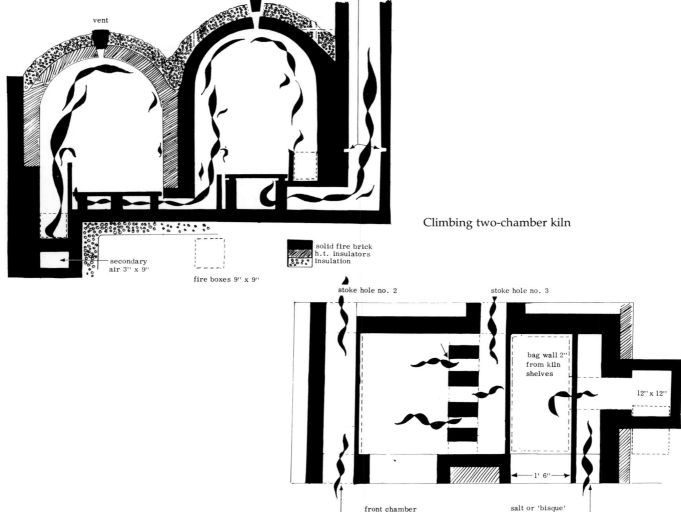

Front Plan

vent

vent

damper slot

secondary air 3" x 9"

fire boxes 9" x 9"

solid fire brick
h.t. insulators
insulation

Climbing two-chamber kiln

stoke hole no. 2

stoke hole no. 3

bag wall 2" from kiln shelves

12" x 12"

1' 6"

front chamber

salt or 'bisque' chamber

stoke hole no. 1

stoke hole no. 4

View inside a gas kiln built from HTI bricks showing floor, flue and internal chimney.

Internal flue of a gas kiln.

## Fuels

### Solid and liquid fuels

Liquid fuels such as oil and bottled gas are very popular because they are easy to obtain and store and they are versatile in that they can be used for firing at all temperatures. An added advantage is that they are relatively clean burning, labour saving in that they obviate the need for stoking, and leave no remaining ash in the fire boxes or as they move through the chamber during firing.

Natural and bottled gas, such as propane or butane, use standard burners, mixers and controls to regulate the amount of heat given off. This fuel is a clean and efficient way with which to fire the kiln. The burner works on the principle of passing gas through a tube fitted with a device to control the flow. It then mixes with air as it enters the burner and is ignited at the other end. An oxidising or reducing flame can be produced with a high degree of control and this fuel used in conjunction with the modern ceramic fibre kiln constructions can be both efficient and economic. One problem that can occur when using bottled gas is that if there is a large quantity drawn off to keep the burners at their maximum output, the tanks can begin to develop ice in the form of frosting at the bottom. This is due to the speed with which liquid fuel converts to a gas. This can be alleviated by linking several tanks together so that less is taken from each at any one time. Another remedy is to run a constant trickle of cold water over the tanks to help them thaw out and prevent this icing up.

### Oil

Oil is a very versatile fuel for both medium-sized and large kilns. The fire mouth needs to be larger than that for gas firing if the fuel is to burn efficiently. For this reason, very small chambers are not very practical for oil burners. Most oil burners work on a mixture of gravity-fed fuel and forced air produced either by a rotary vane compressor or a simple blower fan. The air and fuel are mixed in the burner head and the atomised mixture is ignited. There are various primitive burner systems that use a drip feed mixture where the oil drops onto a hot plate and is then ignited as it vaporises. These are fairly inefficient and as is the case when using most

Gas burners.

Oil pipe work *in situ*.

## Wood and other solid fuels

Wood and other solid fuels are in some ways a very exciting means of firing but they are hard work, very labour intensive and require a great deal of space. The kilns and fire boxes need to be large enough to be efficient, that is to allow full combustion of the fuels and for ease of stoking. Chimneys must also be of an adequate size to create enough draw through the chamber as well as to pull oxygen in with the burning fuel. There are however some very efficient smaller kilns that can be built. For instance, there is the fast fire wood kiln designed by Fred Olsen. Plans for this appear in both his book and mine on kiln building (see Bibliography). Most kiln structures can be lined with ceramic fibre to improve their insulating qualities and fuel economy. This material however does not withstand the corrosive attack of fly ash and other gases as well as a conventional fire brick kiln.

Wood firing is certainly worth considering as an option to the more customary fuels. Rich results can often be obtained from the fly ash deposits and the toasted look of unglazed clay surfaces. This firing method requires a great deal of skill and management in order to coax the kiln to the necessary temperature. This can only be learned by practice. Each kiln will have its own idiosyncrasies, as well as being affected by the weather and wind when the firing takes place,

simple types of burner, they tend to blow out until the fire boxes are hot enough to prevent this happening. Forced air burners are better. They allow a considerable degree of control over both the air and oil and therefore the atmosphere in the kiln and the temperature rise. The chimney must be of a sufficient size to create enough draught through the chamber to pull the long flame that develops from this fuel up through the setting. There is a certain amount of turbulence created by the combustion and the air entering from both the blowers and the primary and secondary air ports. This can be a real advantage when firing with some techniques such as salt glazing in that it greatly helps to push the vapours through the chamber.

Wood fire box showing fire bars in position.

## Wood Kiln

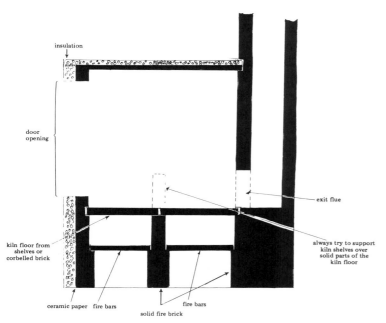

insulation

door
opening

exit flue

kiln floor from
shelves or
corbelled brick

always try to support
kiln shelves over
solid parts of the
kiln floor

ceramic paper   fire bars          fire bars

solid fire brick

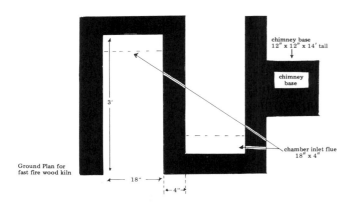

chimney base
12" x 12" x 14' tall

chimney
base

3'

chamber inlet flue
18" x 4"

Ground Plan for
fast fire wood kiln

18"

4"

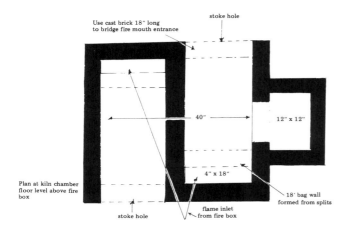

Use cast brick 18" long
to bridge fire mouth entrance

stoke hole

40"

12" x 12"

4" x 18"

Plan at kiln chamber
floor level above fire
box

18' bag wall
formed from splits

stoke hole

flame inlet
from fire box

the condition of the wood and the type that is used. Hardwoods burn more slowly than softwoods and release heat at a steadier rate. Thin cut softwood on the other hand releases its heat very quickly and can be burnt in large quantities so that there must be sufficient space for covered storage and seasoning of the timber.

## Heat Indicators

### Pyrometers

Pyrometers are used to indicate the heat rise within the chamber. They either have a calibrated dial that displays the temperature reading from the attached thermocouple or more recently they have a digital panel that gives the reading in figures. The thermocouple consists of two lengths of metal alloy welded at one end and sheathed in a porcelain tube to protect them. The opposite ends are attached to a galvanometer. The heat in the kiln affects these two metal wires, generating a low voltage electric current that registers on the galvanometer which is calibrated in degrees Celsius. This instrument is very accurate but it only gives a literal reading of the temperature within the chamber and this does not always relate to the amount of heat work that is needed for the glazes to reach maturity. It may take experience and several firings to know when the glazes have reached a good melt and whether they may need to be held for a period at the maximum temperature to soak and develop their best characteristics.

### Pyrometric cones

These are often the most reliable method of knowing exactly what is happening within the chamber. They are made up from a mixture of ceramic materials that melt in a specified cycle and are calibrated in such a way that they bend after a sufficient amount of heat work has taken place in the chamber. This gives a much more realistic indication of the true nature of what is happening inside the kiln. In some special circumstances these cones can read a little off their coded temperature especially if the initial stages of the firing are very fast or in the case of salt firings when the volatilised sodium affects their outer surface. On the whole however they can be relied upon to give accurate readings and should be placed so that they are clearly visible from the spy holes. It always pays to put several of these cone plaques in various parts of the chamber during the first firings to help identify any hot or cold spots. The usual method is to set them in a row of three, the first to melt and indicate when the chamber is nearing the optimum temperature, the second to show when the clay and glazes have matured and the third as a guard cone to warn against over-firing. (A list of cones and their temperature equivalents can be found on p. 155.)

## Loading and Packing

In some primitive kilns the wares were often piled on top of each other or stacked inside refractory saggers to fill the chamber. Modern kilns are now packed using high alumina shelves or batts separated by kiln props made from similar materials. These should be covered with a wash to protect them from glaze drips and other damage. Below is a typical batt wash recipe:

### Batt wash recipe
  3 parts hydrated alumina
  1 part ball clay

Mix the ingredients to a milky consistency and brush or spray the wash onto the upper face of the kiln shelf. It is not advisable to coat the underside as it may flake off during the firings and fall onto the work below. Props can be dipped into this mixture and then again while still wet each end can be dipped into powdered alumina to give them further protection from sticking to the shelving.

### Setting

The weight of a setting of shelves and wares can be considerable so the lower part of the stack must be strong enough to support those above. Three props are always the best arrangement to assure a firmly rigid support. The next layer should always be positioned immediately above those below to prevent undue stress on each shelf. The whole arrangement should never be allowed to become unstable since there is always a certain amount of movement within the kiln, especially at high temperatures, as the chamber and wares expand and contract with the heat. Weaknesses in the early stages of packing could cause the bank of shelves to twist or collapse with disastrous results.

In the case of an electric firing kiln, the lower areas of the chamber can be packed closely both for economic reasons and also to allow radiated heat to pass from one part of the setting to the other. Tall work is often better placed at the top of the chamber. However, whatever the setting, always try to place items of a uniform size on each shelf to keep the pack as tight as possible.

If you are using four props which will sometimes be necessary in the case of very heavy shelves, always make sure that there is no movement or wobble. If there is, it can be adjusted by the use of thin sections of broken refractory shelving placed on top of a prop or by a mix of alumina and grogged clay wedged into any gap. A typical recipe for a wadding mix is given below. Small variations in shelf height can be changed in the same way if a little clearance is needed over the top of a row of work. The pack can be continued in this manner until the kiln is loaded.

### Wadding mix recipe
  2 parts China clay
  8 parts hydrated alumina
  1 part ball clay
  1 part grog
  1 part flour

The plain flour acts as a binding agent for the rest of the ingredients. This material can be rolled into balls and placed under the work to lift it clear of the kiln shelves and prevent snagging or running glaze causing damage.

If draw rings are to be used in the firing to test the glaze melt and amount of reduction, then these must be placed in a position so that they can be easily lifted out with a metal rod through the spy hole. This is most important in the case of salt firings when such draw trials are essential to evaluate the amount of glaze build-up within the chamber. Once the packing is finished and all is complete, the door can be closed or bricked up, insulated and clammed with fireclay to fill any gaps in readiness to start the firing.

Crouching figure (by Author) *in situ* on kiln base.

## Firing

### Bisque firing

This initial firing is begun when the wares packed in the chamber are completely dry. Start on a very slow, gentle heat rise to allow any steam from water retained in the clay to escape, probably at around 100°C. This stage should never be rushed. It is important to ensure that there is adequate time for the moisture content to clear without creating undue pressure within the clay which could cause it to burst. If in any doubt, hold a small mirror over the flue and see if there is any condensation on the glass. This will indicate if any water is still being given off.

Having reached this point, the rate of temperature climb should not exceed 100° an hour

until the next important stage is reached. This is between 300°C and 500°C when the chemically combined water will begin to be driven off. This is the point when the clay particles are drawn closer together and the material is changed into a strong and solid form. The free silica also increases in volume in what is known as the alpha beta conversion. Another reaction is also start-

Fibre kiln with top in position.

Flue vent in roof of ceramic fibre kiln.

Figure in position in ceramic fibre kiln.

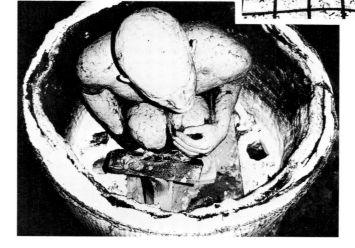

ing to take place at this time: the beta quartz is beginning to be affected by the temperature rise and it is slowly converting to beta cristobalite and increasing in volume yet again. This change is not complete in that not all the beta quartz converts at the same time. That part that does convert becomes irreversible, but the remainder can change in the cooling cycle to alpha quartz and begin to contract. This can cause dunting and cracking of the fired clay if this stage is allowed to happen too fast. Once the chamber has reached this point the firing can be speeded up until the bisque temperature is reached at anything from 1000°C to 1100°C. During this time any organic matter is burnt off and the alkalis in the mixture will react with the alumina and silica present to sinter and begin to fuse the body together. Once the optimum temperature is reached, the kiln can be left to cool or soaked for a period of oxidation to clear away any carbon deposits that may be present if solid fuel has been used.

When firing very large or thick work for the first time, wrap the piece in a layer of fibre blanket to ensure that it does not heat up unevenly especially if the burners are in a position where the heat will strike the unfired clay at one particular point before reaching the rest of the work. If this should happen, great stress can build up and cause warping or cracking. Problems may also arise when applying glazes on unevenly fired surfaces.

## Glaze Firing Techniques

### Sawdust firing

This is perhaps one of the more primitive ways of firing but some very unexpected and interesting results can be obtained from trapped carbon, reduction and oxidation marks, flame flashing and, of course, wood ash deposits which occur with this method.

The technique is to begin by spreading a base of sawdust or combustible materials in a shallow trough in the ground along with some larger pieces of wood. The wares are then placed onto this layer and covered with more sawdust, and so on, building layer upon layer. Old chicken wire can be placed between each successive layer to prevent those above falling on and cracking the ones below as the fuel burns away. The outside of the heap can be built up with

bricks to help contain the pots and materials in some organised shape. A little paraffin should be poured over the top layer to help ignite the sawdust. Once it is smouldering satisfactorily, the whole construction can be covered with a sheet of corrugated iron. This will help protect the heap from the wind which can cause the combustible materials to burn too rapidly and crack the pieces. A slow steady burning is the best means of gaining good, even results. Smaller experiments can be undertaken using a garden bonfire or one of those small metal incinerators used for the disposal of garden refuse.

Burnished surfaces which have been fired in this method can be very attractive. So too, are those that have been pre-stained with slips and oxides. Other materials such as soluble copper can be introduced into the sawdust to further enhance the surfaces. Salt can also either be combined with the combustible materials or sprinkled directly onto the surfaces of the wares to add to the texture and colour of the fired clay. The process is not one that can be controlled with any degree of accuracy but this is half the charm and excitement of this method.

### Raku kilns

There are many ways to build a simple kiln for use at this temperature. They can be made from either common bricks, fire bricks, HTIs or other materials such as ceramic fibre. The former tend to be a little primitive and wasteful on fuel but they have one advantage in that they can be built in the open air and the fire boxes made big enough to burn solid fuels. The fibre and HTIs are easily and quickly fired with bottled gas and can be made portable or in sections that can be added one to another to enlarge the chamber size when needed. The choice of kiln will therefore be determined by the size and shape of the work to be fired in it and the availability of fuel.

A small wood-burning kiln as described in my book on kiln building (see Bibliography) is easily and quickly put together and can be constructed from any sort of brick. The structure is built up from a level foundation covered with sand or concrete. There is no need for the bricks to be mortared together. They can simply be laid dry one on the other to form a simple fire box, chamber and base for a chimney that can be further extended with a length of steel tube to give it the height needed for a good draught.

## Raku Kiln

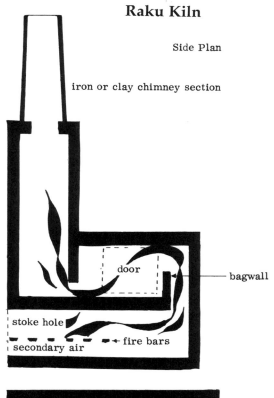

iron or clay chimney section

door

bagwall

stoke hole

secondary air — fire bars

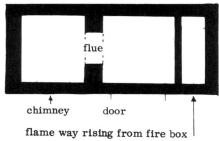

flue

chimney — door

flame way rising from fire box

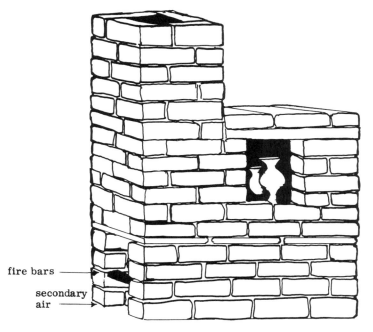

fire bars

secondary air

The work is removed from the chamber through the opening in the side, which can be covered with a kiln shelf or ceramic fibreboard to act as a door.

A simple ceramic fibre raku kiln can be constructed as follows:

Form a circle from either a fine gauge chicken wire or heavier gauge steel mesh. Both can be strengthened by strong wire rings attached at the top and bottom to help keep the shape rigid. This wire tube is then lined with ceramic fibre blanket attached to the framework by means of stitches of nichrome wire pushed through the

Slabbed raku dish by John Kershaw.
Photograph by Andrew Morris.

blanket and twisted through the mesh. A small aperture should be cut in the side near the base to allow the burner to be inserted at the bottom of the chamber. The foundation can be made from any bricks available to form a rough platform for the structure and covered with another layer of fibre blanket for additional insulation. The roof of the kiln is made in much the same way as the walls; a circle of wire mesh cut to the diameter of the top of the chamber can have a layer of blanket stitched to it or it could be made from a section of ceramic fibreboard cut to the required size. Access to the chamber can either be through this top opening or the complete

95

chamber can be lifted and removed from the base section.

An even more durable framework can be made from an old oil drum (that has had the bottom cut out) lined with fibre glued in position with an adhesive that can be purchased from most fibre suppliers. A small hole should be provided at the top to act as a flue allowing heat and gases to escape as needed. There should also be suitable arrangements at the base to provide access to the burners and a level platform for the body of the kiln.

### Post-raku firing

This is usually done when the work is removed from the kiln at the stage when the glaze is molten. Using tongs the item is picked up and transferred to a container filled with combustible materials such as sawdust or leaves that have been slightly dampened. The results of this form of local reduction are not always completely predictable but once the process has been worked with and a known set of variables are followed each time, the effects can be controlled to a degree. Always take precautions against possible accidents such as loose clothing that could catch on fire. Wear protective gloves and make sure that the work area is clear of any unnecessary obstructions.

Having removed the object from the chamber and placed it in the reduction material, make sure that the smoke produced can clear from the work area without delaying the progress of the rest of the activity. Once the reduction cycle has been completed, the work can be removed and checked. If the effects on the clay and glaze are

Wood fire stoke hole for raku brick kiln.

Brick built raku kiln, two drying chambers built on top to use waste heat to dry glaze off before fusing and to preheat the work.

Small, bottle-gas-fired raku kiln made from wire frame and ceramic fibre.

satisfactory, it can be left to air cool or be placed into a container filled with water to freeze the results of the reduction. Should the work be very large or too heavy to move using tongs, then the body of the kiln must be lifted clear of the base and replaced with another section over

Vessel by Sebastian Blackie.

the still red hot work. The reduction material is then quickly poured into this second container, surrounding and covering the piece. If necessary, it can be sealed with a lid to cut down the oxygen supply and slow the burning rate. A simple chicken wire frame can be made up for this purpose, in the same manner as the kiln. The inner face and the lid can be lined with several layers of metal foil to make the chamber air tight. This is both light and easy to move into position, which is a great advantage when working in these very hot and tense conditions. It is possible to dispense with this last method by merely removing the lid of the chamber and, having extinguished the burners, pouring the reduction materials directly over the work *in situ*.

### Earthenware kilns

There are many possible variations of kiln types for this firing temperature. The standard electric kiln is the most widely used but other solid fuel burning types can be brought into service both for firing in oxidising atmospheres or, if it is required, reduction. They can be built in all the usual materials, brick or fibre, and fired with a number of different fuels. The modern electric designs are both efficient and economical on fuel consumption and perhaps do the least amount of damage to the atmosphere in the way of pollution, bearing in mind that electricity is generated in some cases by the burning of fossil fuels and even in some cases by the use of nuclear reactors.

Firings can be relatively trouble free in these modern electric kilns, effortless and economical, utilising modern technology to ensure the best results, especially when combined with multi-ramp pre-programmed electronic temperature control devices that work in conjunction with pyrometers to give very complete control over temperature rise, soaking periods and other aspects of the firing cycle.

A simple form of gas kiln can be made for use at this temperature in the same manner as that described for raku firings using ceramic fibre (see p. 93). It can be made in various proportions to suit the size and shape of the wares to be fired. The chamber can be loaded through the top, built up with shelves and props to form the best setting. If necessary the chamber can be made in a square section instead of circular as described to facilitate the use of conventional rectangular batts.

### Oxidation and reduction

The conditions present in the chamber during the firing cycle will effect the final colour and texture of both the body and the glaze. At temperatures above 800°C in an electric kiln very few changes take place unless some organic material is deliberately introduced into the chamber or the glaze mix. This means that the atmosphere remains neutral. Raw flame kilns can be starved of oxygen at various stages of the firing to create a reduction atmosphere. Kilns of this type require a considerable amount of oxygen to cause complete combustion and if the fuel supply is increased and the air supply reduced then the atmosphere inside the kiln will become laden with unburnt particles of fuel and carbon. This can be controlled further by the opening and closing of the flues at the base of the chimney by the use of a damper plate to slow down the pull of flame and heat through the chamber and in consequence the amount of air passing through the fire mouths around the burner ports. Adjustments to both of these will vary from kiln to kiln and only practice and experience will give the required amount of reduction. Any of these methods will create a certain amount of smoke and toxic fumes which must be evacuated away from the studio by means of

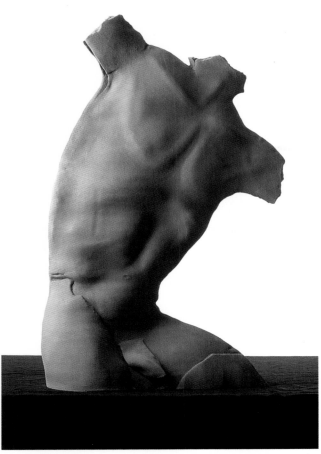

'Black Eugene' by Christie Brown, 30" high, 18" wide and 7" deep. Fired at 1160°C, smoked and waxed.

takes place. Iron-bearing materials for example will be affected considerably since in its usual state of ferric oxide it is red in colour but in reduction it turns into black iron oxide. This reaction changes the colour of both the body, making it darker and flecked with iron spots if it has iron present, and the glaze changing the normal oxidised colouring from the lighter colours of creams, tans and yellows to blues and greens. The more saturated mixes that give dark browns to blacks in oxidation will be mainly unaffected except that they may appear richer and speckled with other iron reds and blacks.

It is possible to introduce materials into an electric kiln to cause reduction; small slivers of wood or moth balls can be pushed through spy holes to create a smoke laden atmosphere. This can have a damaging effect on the electric elements and it may need several firings in oxidation between each reduction to help prevent too much deterioration. Another method that gives good localised reduction is to place work in saggers with combustible materials packed around them and sealed to prevent oxygen entering. A similar but new technique is to wrap the object in layers of slightly dampened newspaper and then cover this completely with tin baking foil, leaving a small air gap between the two. The outer layer of foil should be sealed as well as possible, to help trap the carbon produced from the burning paper inside the envelope.

### Stoneware kilns

High firing temperatures need kilns that are well insulated and built from materials that are able to withstand the stresses and strains put on them from constant heating and cooling. Most modern kilns available on the market are built from ceramic fibreboard and fibre blanket in combination with a high temperature insulation back up. They can be fired using electricity or gas to give clean and efficient oxidising atmospheres as well as reducing conditions by those that burn solid fuels. The simple fibre updraught kiln that was described for the previous two temperature ranges can also be used for the production of stoneware. The basic kiln structure remains the same but instead of a single layer of blanket the inner surface should be lined with a grade high enough to withstand up to

a chimney or other suitable ventilation system.

Reduction of the clay body is normally begun at around 1000°C before the glaze surface begins to melt and seal the surface. The objective is to maintain a steady medium atmosphere from this point onward. Too much smoke can cause carbon to become trapped in the clay as the temperature rises and this can produce blistering and other problems. What is happening is that the flame is being starved of oxygen and seeks out any oxygen particles in the materials that make up the wares in the kiln both from the clay and oxides present. This alters the chemical composition of the wares and causes their colour to change and darken. Later as the glazes melt in the same type of atmosphere, a similar reaction

'The Horn of Plenty is Empty' by Anthony Theakston, 7" × 7".
Terra sigillata, press moulded.

1300°C. The second layer can be a lower grade and it acts as an added insulated back-up to the hot face. The size and shape of a chamber built in this manner are only limited by the number of burners used and their heat output. The taller and narrower the kiln, the more likely it is that there will be a variation of temperature between the top and bottom. This can be controlled to a certain extent by opening and closing the size of the exit flue to either let heat out or contain it. It may take several firings to the able to evaluate this and make any adjustments necessary to get the best balance. However this type of kiln will always have a tendency to be hotter at the top when fired to temperatures above 1150°C.

An alteration of the same structure can be made to turn this type of kiln into a down-draught kiln by inserting an internal sleeve to act as a chimney. This can be made up from a section of blanket formed into a narrow tube with an opening at the bottom to vent the gases out and away at the top. Obviously the size of the internal chimney and the exit flue will vary according to the measurements of the chamber and the burner size.

## Glaze Firing Techniques

These firings are governed by the temperature at which the glaze melts and the type of technique being employed, ranging from low temperature lustres from 700°C through to raku, earthen-ware, stoneware and porcelain at 1300°C.

Unlike the first bisque firing when work can be stacked closely together or on top of one another, those in the glaze firing must be placed so that they do not touch and are prevented from sticking to the kiln shelves as the glazes melt. This can be done by applying a batt wash made up from a mix of alumina and China clay (see p. 92) painted on or sprayed over the kiln furniture, and by the use of stilts or bars to keep the bases of the work free of the shelves. Small circles of ceramic fibre paper placed under the wares not only help to prevent this problem but also separate the two surfaces and allow any further contraction to take place as the clay shrinks at higher temperatures thereby preventing the problem of bases cracking or snagging as they contract.

The initial stages of a glaze firing should be started slowly to allow any moisture to clear from the glaze and bisqued clay especially if the work is thick and heavy. So, a slow steady increase of heat should be aimed for until a temperature is reached around 500°C when the rate of climb can be increased to whatever is considered satisfactory to reach the optimum temperature.

When firing to stoneware temperatures all the items in the kiln should be checked to make sure that they are stable on the shelves and that there is no possibility of any of them falling or moving in such way that they can come into contact either with one another or any of the kiln shelves or props. Spurs and other measures used in lower temperature firings can cause problems of warping and distortion at these higher temperatures so a firm base and flat shelf surface should always be found if at all possible. Sand or grog can be used as well as the ceramic paper mentioned before to allow the bases of each piece to contract easily as they shrink in the latter part of the firing and become vitrified. In the case of special techniques such as salt glazing, there are other ways of treating both the kiln furniture and the bases of the individual work to help prevent these problems. A wadding can be made to raise the foot of a piece of work free from the shelf. This can be rolled out to form coils or pads to support the wares. It is also useful as a means of separating sections that need to be kept apart. This mixture is also useful in a conventional stoneware glaze firing to keep the bases clear of kiln shelves that have become old and warped or damaged from drips of glaze from past firings.

### Salt firing

The basic principle of this technique is to introduce salt into the chamber at temperatures around 1220°C and upwards. The reaction that takes place is that the salt changes under the conditions of heat, breaking down into its component parts, sodium and chlorine. The chlorine gas is expelled from the chamber into the atmosphere and the remaining sodium reacts with the silica in the clay to form a glass-like covering over everything in the kiln. This affects the

Small gas-fired salt kiln similar to the one described below.

whole of the chamber as well and all the interior shelves, props and walls. Kilns therefore tend to be built from solid materials such as fire bricks, or castable high alumina cement and aggregates as these materials are relatively unaffected by the vapour. High temperature insulation bricks are too soft and porous for this purpose because the salt vapour can leach into the brickwork through the open texture and destroy them very quickly unless they are coated with a protective layer to prevent this corrosion. The nature of this technique is that the kiln improves when it has been fired several times and the amount of salt used can be reduced after the initial firings. This is because a certain quantity of salt remains in the fire boxes and other parts of the structure to revolatilise each time the kiln gets hot enough. Some experiments have been done using the high alumina ceramic blanket for salt kilns but this tends to become brittle and likely to flake and break down quite quickly. It also

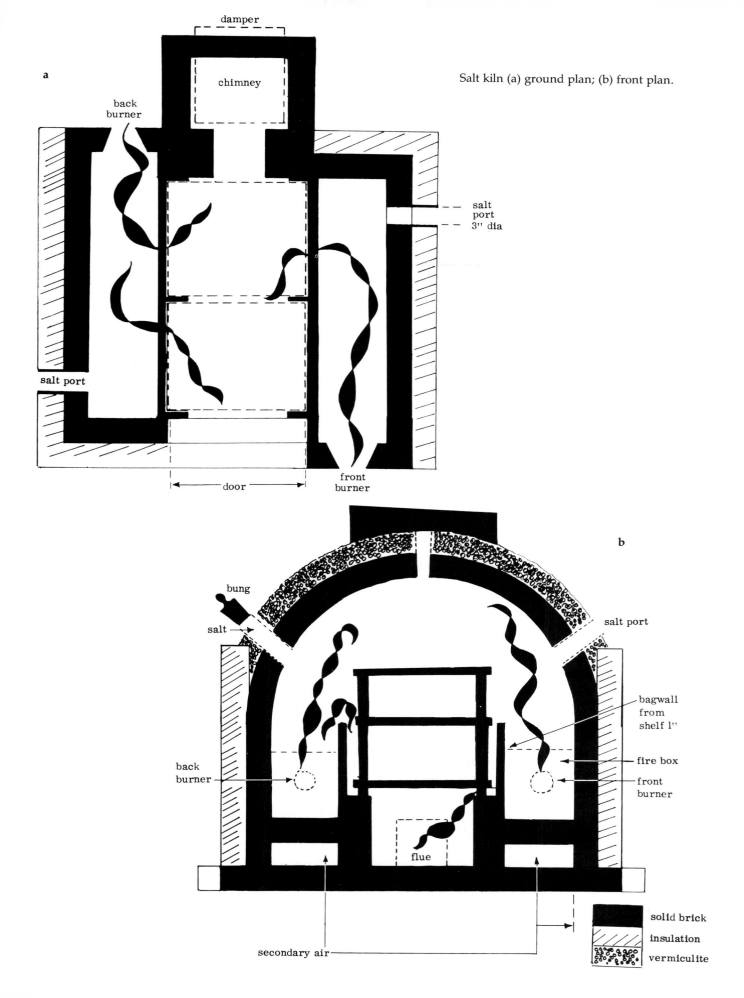

Salt kiln (a) ground plan; (b) front plan.

a

damper

chimney

back
burner

salt
port
3" dia

salt port

door

front
burner

b

bung

salt

salt port

back
burner

bagwall
from
shelf 1"

fire box

front
burner

flue

secondary air

solid brick

insulation

vermiculite

does not allow for any build up of residual salt to remain after the firing and this means that large quantities of salt will have to be used each time the kiln is charged.

The average quantity of salt for the first few firings in a kiln built of solid materials is about one pound for every cubic foot of kiln space. Another factor worth pointing out is that when the dampened salt is introduced into the chamber not only does the temperature drop and slow the firing process but there is also a build up of pressure from steam and vapour. Great care must be taken that the structure is secure and no damage can occur, and that the gases that are emitted from firing ports and expansion joints are not inhaled. **Always wear a mask, goggles and protective gloves when introducing the salt as it can spit back through open ports and cause burns to the eyes and hands.**

Almost all salt kilns have a relatively short lifespan in relation to other stoneware kilns since the corrosive action of the salt attacks the brickwork quite quickly and weakens the structure. Iron work used to support the arch and other parts of the chamber are prone to rusting quickly so all of these should be checked at regular intervals between firings for any weakness that might develop.

Close-up of a piece of raku by Paul Soldner.
Low salt and fire flashing. Photograph by Stephen Brayne.

## Firing Times

These will obviously vary from firing to firing as some packs will be lighter or denser than others depending on the nature and shape of the individual pieces. These variations will not only effect the time that it takes for the kiln to reach temperature but also in the case of solid fuels the flame patterns within the chamber.

It follows therefore, that the more shelves and denser the pack in each setting, the greater amount of heat will be needed to get the kiln to temperature. Furthermore if the kiln is out of doors then the air temperature will have some effect on the firing pattern. The prevailing wind may also determine the pull on the chimney to a greater or lesser extent. It is always worth keeping a kiln log on each firing, making careful notes as to all the possible variations each time a firing is undertaken. These can be listed under headings as follows:

**Time**
7am
**Temperature**
100°C
**Burner Control Setting**
One on low full air
**Atmosphere**
oxidizing
**Remarks**
steady

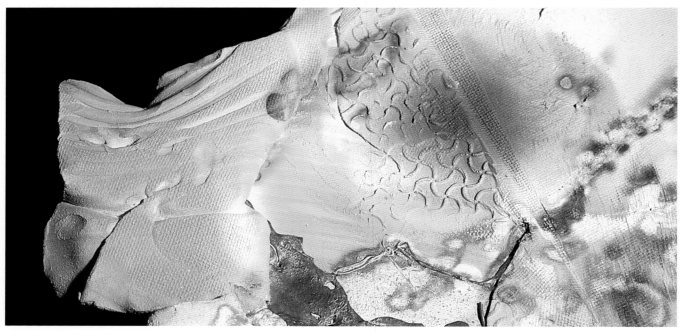

## Faults During Firing

There are a number of problems that can develop during the firing process and these show themselves in various ways. Some faults only become evident after the process has been finished and can be attributed to either bad making methods or some of the following.

### Cracks

Hair-line or wide cracks can be caused in the initial stages of the heating process by raising the temperature too fast and the same thing can happen in the cooling cycle if the fall in temperature is too rapid.

If the object has a glazed surface and this appears to have merged over the break, it can be safely assumed that the crack is due to splitting in the early stages as the temperature increases allowing the glaze to melt over the edges of the damaged area. If, on the other hand, the break is fresh looking in that it is clean and sharp edged, then this has most likely happened when the kiln has been cooled. Free silica present can be one of the reasons for this problem developing and may necessitate an adjustment of the original body mix or the slowing down of the firing cycle at the critical stages of 100°C and 500°C to 600°C.

### Spalling

This is when small areas of the work either crack and fall away or the entire object explodes in the kiln. Both are due to the fact that there is still water in the clay body and that a full and satisfactory drying has not occurred before the initial heating. The obvious solution is to extend the time allowed for this process before attempting to bisque the wares. Another measure is to slow the firing down to give ample time for any steam to escape in the early stages, especially if the work is thick. In some cases it may even be necessary to open the body mix with further additions of grog and other agents to ensure that it is of the correct consistency to allow any contained water to clear at these early stages of the process. If the object is an enclosed form in that there are spaces inside where there is no movement of air to facilitate the steady progress of drying, then prolonged periods may be needed to ensure that the item is ready to fire.

Splits and spalls of this type can also occur

from the reduced iron in the body which changed to iron sulphide during the bisque firing. This can react with any water present to form a gas strong enough when expanded to blow a section of the wall away. Calcium deposits can also cause the same reaction. When cooling they can pick up water from the atmosphere and cause an expansion of part of the piece. This can be enough to put pressure in a particular, localised area to make that section expand and break away.

### Black core

This may occur when thick items are fired too fast causing the clay to behave in the following manner. The body develops a dark grey or black core that weakens it. One reason for this is that the clay mix is too tight or dense without enough openers so that the gases are prevented from escaping. A second possibility is that the iron present in the clay is reduced and is not able to oxidise properly. It then begins to behave as a flux and vitrifies at temperatures far below normal. This problem however usually only affects those clays that are high in iron, especially fine red earthenware types.

### Warping

Warping is often caused by forced or uneven drying or other faults in the making process, such as the putting together of clay sections that are at different stages of drying. This problem can also develop during firing because of the position of the object in the kiln. For instance, if one side of a piece is affected by flame pattern or by receiving more heat in a concentrated area than the other, uneven shrinkage will occur. Setting a piece of work on unstable or lopsided supports can also produce stress that can affect the clay in a similar way, causing it to lose its shape, especially when firing at high temperatures.

### Bloating

Bloating appears as unsightly blisters on the surface of a piece. It is often caused by overfiring particularly in the case of earthenware clays. With stoneware, bloating can occur when gases are formed within the clay after the surface has become sealed because the heat rise from 800°C to 1000°C has happened too fast. In some other cases, it can also appear if there were foreign materials in the original mixing of the clay body or if the reduction process has been too heavy.

### Efflorescence

In some earthenware body mixes and indeed in other types that contain high iron percentages, there is another problem that can affect the final finished appearance of the surface. This is commonly referred to as efflorescence. It is most noticed as a scumming over the basic body colour. It is caused by calcium sulphate and other ingredients such as magnesium that remain soluble and do not combine with the materials that make up the body mix. It can be cured by the remixing of the body clay with the addition of barium carbonate which is stable in its insoluble form. It will not react with moisture and becomes integrated with the other materials of the body clay. Firing to a higher temperature will in some cases also clear this unwanted white powdery scum from the surface, especially if the work is soaked at the end of the firing for a period long enough to allow the sulphates to become thoroughly combined and no longer soluble.

'Vehicle Man' by Gary Wornell, height 25cm.
Terracotta slips, lithium carbonate glazes and multiple firings were used on this piece.

## Care and Safety

Whichever method is used in firing, it must always be realised that a kiln contains a very considerable amount of heat and is potentially dangerous. Kilns should always be checked from time to time in order to ensure that they are in good condition and safe to use. The possibility of burns from hot fire boxes, burner equipment and spy bricks should never be overlooked. Fuel lines should be checked on a regular basis and care taken not to allow any combustible materials to be left near the kiln when a firing is in progress. Clothing should be worn that is not likely to catch on surrounding objects, long hair should be tied back as it can easily scorch when looking through spy holes. Never under estimate the amount of reflected heat from burner ports and when stoking fire boxes with highly combustible fuels. Eyes should always be protected when looking into the chamber at any stage of the firing even when not very hot. A blow back from a change of wind direction could have disasterous effects. Asbestos gloves should also be worn to protect hands from the conducted heat retained by spy bungs, fire box doors, burners, damper plates and other items around the firing area. Finally, always keep a fire extinguisher near at hand whenever a firing is in progress!

Above
Form by Colin Pearson.
Stoneware, thrown and altered with applied additions.
Below
'Blue and Bronze Tray' by John Chalke, 28 × 17 × 9 cm.
Press moulded with barium and manganese glazes with
gold film; fired to cone 6 and cone 018.

Above
'Going Back' by John Chalke, 35 × 24 × 11 cm.
Three layered piece: thrown stoneware with manganese-
alumina slip, distorted on edge in wood kiln. Dinnerware
shard fired onto back and pierced with diamond drill;
bronze glazed third layer fired onto back of shard. Cone
10 and cone 6 firings.

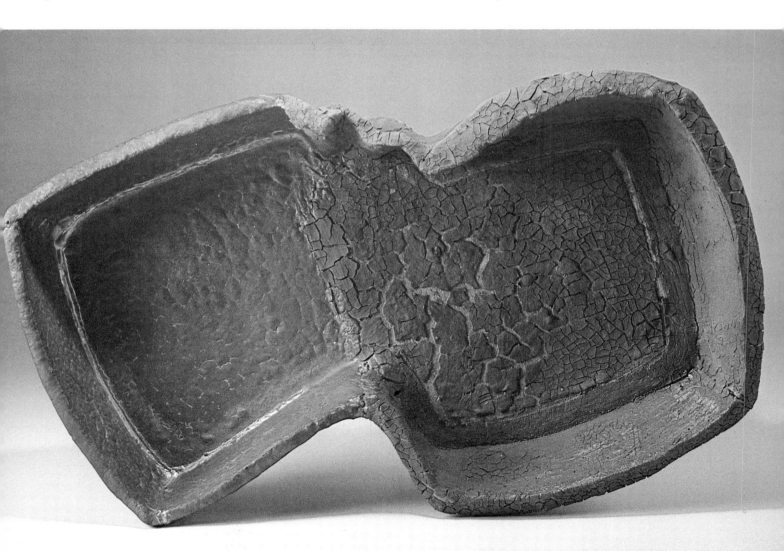

Left
Slab form by Jim Robison.
Fired stoneware slab form.

Below
Teapot by Gary Wornell, height 45 cm.
Terra sigillata, slab built.

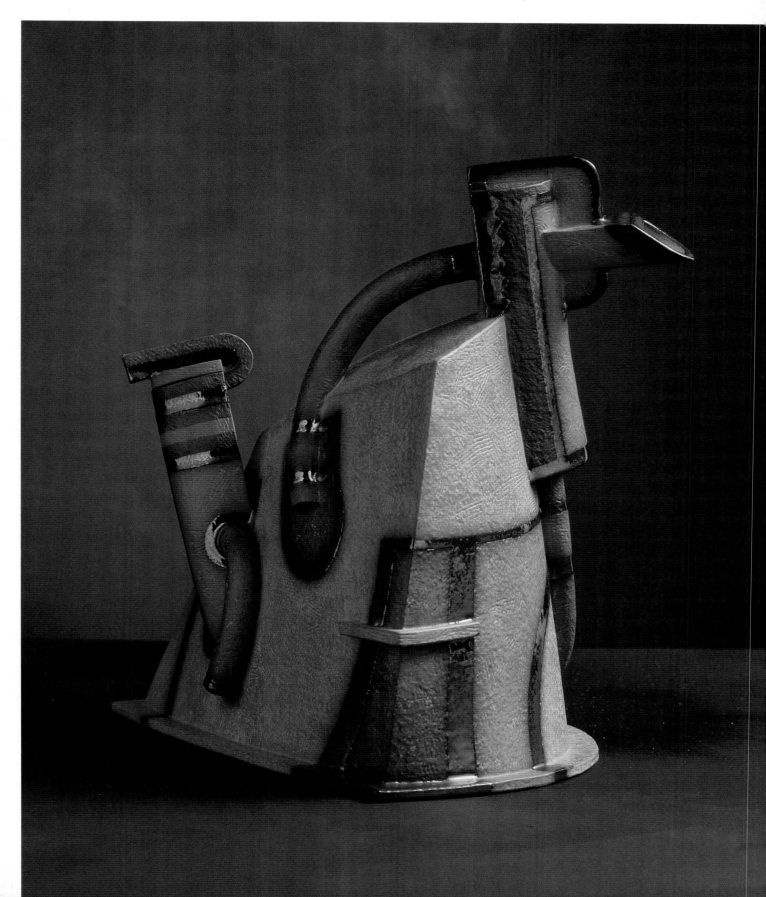

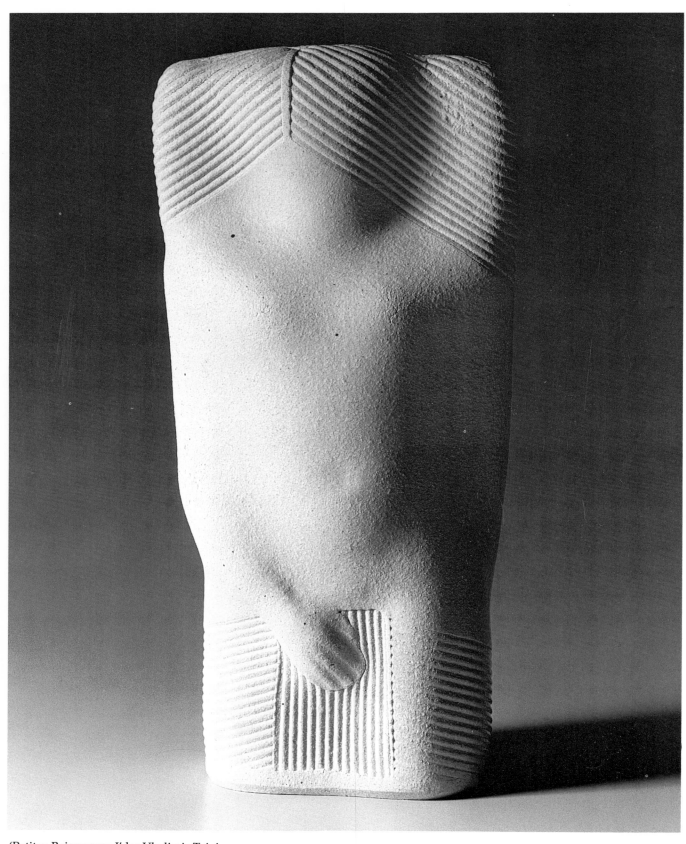

'Petites Baigneuses I' by Vladimir Tsivin.
Porcelain.

Above
'Fallen Angel Triptych' by Mark Stanczyk.
Slab built.

Right
'Fallen Angel Excavation' by Mark Stanczyk.

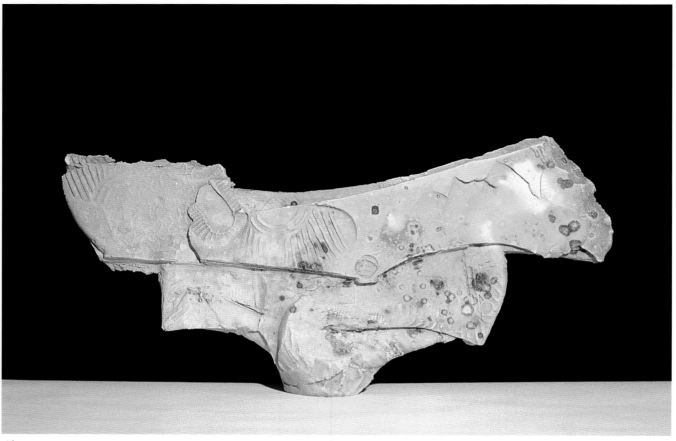

Above
Raku figure by Paul Soldner.
Low salt fired raku. Photograph by Stephen Brayne.

Below
Boat sculpture by Peter Phillips.
Reduced stoneware, matt glazed, 9″ × 9″.

'Gothic flowers' by John Maltby, 12″ × 9″ wide. Vase with over handle. Stoneware, painted clay and glaze.

Above
'Autumn Breeze', marquette for monument, by Michael
Flynn, height 14". Stoneware.

Below
Spouted form by David Scott.
Slab built earthenware.

Right
Object by Michael Bayley.
Unglazed, fired to 1250 – 1280°C St Thomas body,
chocolate black, grog and sand.

Below
'The Mechanical Bride' by Anthony Theakston, 36″ × 25″.
Press moulded earthenware polished 'Zeebrite' surface.

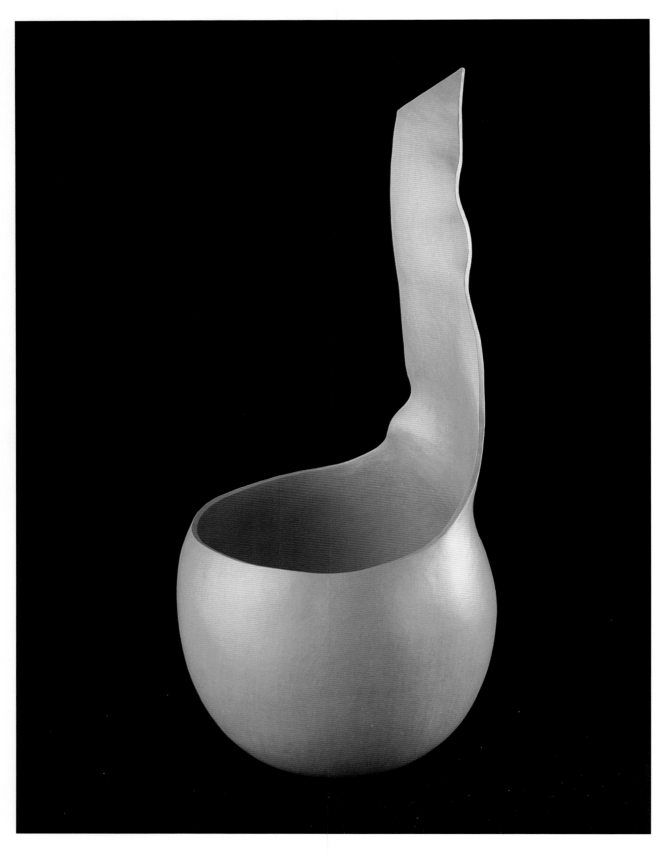

Vessels by Tina Vlassopulos.
Handbuilt, burnished earthenware.

Above
'Deux Femmes' by Philip Eglin.
Earthenware figures, slabbed and modelled.

Left
Vessel form by Monica Young, 4'10" – 5' tall.
Coil built stoneware.

'Exquisite Nomads' by Xavier Toubes.
Handbuilt and coiled, multi-fired between 1100°C and
900°C.

# Profiles of Some Modern Ceramicists

## *Michel Kuipers*

The work of Michel Kuipers is sculptural in character and concerned with the philosophical content. His work is closely linked with the present developments in modern art and in particular the fundamentalism where the emphasis is on the process as well as on the properties of the materials.

In the past he was concerned with the breaking and tearing of the clay and the reconstruction of these developed fragments into the form of straight lines, circles or squares. These works express his interest in archaeology and the deterioration processes that have taken place over centuries in such finds. These are linked to his ceramic objects by the means of rough unglazed broken surfaces contrasting strongly with a smooth, glazed and decorated adjoining areas. The artist expresses, thus, the contrast between nature and cultivation. This theme is explored further in the 1980s in compositions where amorphous, raw clay fragments are confronted with smooth, glazed geometrical forms.

Recently his work consists of huge, monumental sculptures along with a series of much smaller scale pieces that sometimes serve as a sketch for the larger work. Since this period he has also developed a keen interest in the pot form as a theme for sculpture. He reduces the forms to elementary concepts like circumference, height and width modules. Added to these is the handle element that takes on a different meaning, either as elementary remainders of a pot form like the amphora or as a counterbalance within the piece. In many of these recent works he seems to focus in particular on the art of omission. His compositions that exist of elementary parts bring about the illusion of complete forms, for example a rainbow, a staircase, a pot or a human figure. The most spectacular example of this is the bipartite sculpture 'The Walkers' which he recently erected in an urban park in the town of Eindhoven, Netherlands.

Extracts from an article
by Mieke Spruit-Ledeboer

With his work 'The Walkers', Michel Kuipers made it clear that with his feeling for the poetic means of expression available in ceramics, his feeling for balance between the natural elements and cultivated forms and his sense of humour, the real aim of this piece of sculpture is that it be in harmony with its surroundings. His design carried out in his workshop consisted of two forms each about seven feet in height. They are situated opposite each other on the inside of the circular pavement and like the letters of the alphabet, they consist of an inner and an outer form. The inner forms outline two abstract figures walking in opposite directions. Figures that are present and absent at the same time, they are immaterial and leave space between their contours for the surrounding trees, plants and lawns that in these negative forms gain a special meaning for the spectator, sitting on one of the nearby seats.

While the inner form directs towards the concentrated experience of the surroundings, the outer form relaxes in the space that is left. One can interpret these contrasts as mere contemplation of matter and space, or as connections between form elements, thus related and reconstructed so that metaphors like 'Space-container' or 'Face Lift' are created for the spectator. With this in mind standing in front of this new work I couldn't suppress the feeling that the artist had played a trick on me.

Extract from an article written by
Brita Bakema (Holland)

'Dark Circle' by Michel Kuipers, 10.5 × 136 × 154 cm.

Above
'The Walkers' by Michel Kuipers.

Left
'Holding a Secret' by Michel Kuipers, 21.5 × 36 × 59 cm.
Modelled and hollowed out stoneware, reduced and
lustred.

Right
'Rocking Mountains' under construction.

# Irene Vonk

*Irene Vonk says of her work:*

My choice to work with clay in no way means that I feel myself limited to shapes or techniques that are prescribed by ceramics. I use clay in a very immediate way and what I want above all is to make use of the particular qualities of this material – its great plasticity and flexibility.

I try to manipulate the clay as little as possible. I allow it to react directly to every situation and I make use of the traces that I leave in it. I work with separate strips of clay with which I 'paint' a piece of taut canvas using my hand. I later assemble these strips, that you could compare with broad brush strokes of a painter, into three-dimensional 'painted' shapes.

By working with separate pieces I can introduce movement into the final shape, that rhythm in a photographic still. So the very movements determine the final shape.

In my last works I develop something from a solid, soft shape into which I stamp a certain movement. That which took place inside the shape determines the outward shape: movement and shape have become one. The shape is not planned, or predetermined in a traditional manner, it is the result of a physical action. Dance is a major source of inspiration for me. In my work I want to express certain emotions, by means of movement and gesture.

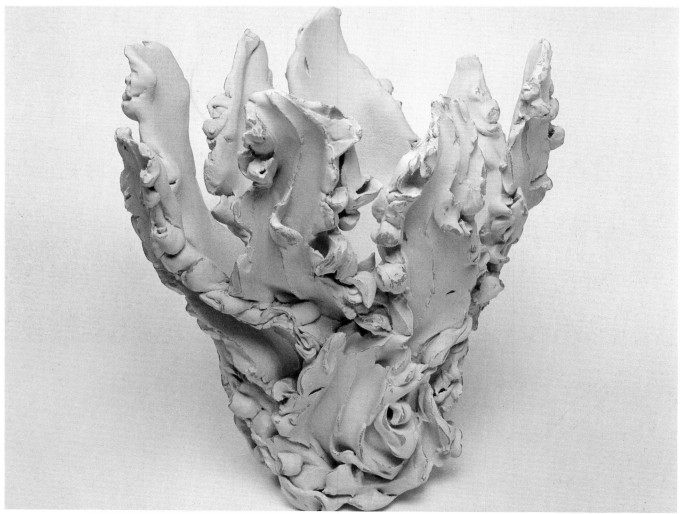

Above
Vase form by Irene Vonk, 60 × 50 cm.
*Rijksdienst Beeldende Kunst collection.*

Left
Vase by Irene Vonk, 40 × 30 × 70 cm.
Modelled and handbuilt.
*Stedelyk Museum collection, Amsterdam.*

## Mo Jupp

In my own work, for some years I have tried to find a style that is instantly recognisable; one that would make my life easier and suit my many needs. This seems to have always eluded me. I have always made functional pieces. Functional in that I always have a particular goal that I am trying to achieve. I start with a check-list and try to find a material and making method to satisfy it. Hence I suppose, my lack of recognisable style. To have a passing knowledge of all the different techniques within the field of ceramics, plus a few from other disciplines and a raging optimism are the cornerstones that allow me to operate fully.

The subject matter that has occupied me since 1978, namely my attitude to the female, has remained fairly constant. The reason for this lengthy preoccupation is that I am always look-ing for better ways to describe what I mean. It is like a conversation that is not being understood. One changes one's tack and puts it another way in the hope of making it clearer.

I spend at least four hours a week in libraries looking at books, magazines and the way other artists have solved their problems. I see my in-volvement with fired clay in this light, namely as a problem-solving exercise. Mostly subjects offer themselves to me, for example, the rise of the feminist movement and the opinions of the young male. I feel that I must make some com-ment, must state my attitude. This is very often not the case. I do not feel like a vessel-maker although I can do it and I do have strong opi-nions. I think that today's potters should address themselves to today's problems. I am very conscious of the 'hollow' and I work within the confines of what I can only call traditional mores, but it came as a big surprise to me to learn that sculptors making life-sized fired fig-ures in the late nineteenth century built their pieces by coiling, not that they called it that though.

I have problems, I try to solve them, how doesn't really matter. I enjoy using clay more than any other material because I can manipu-late it better, I can do what I want. I don't know if I am a sculptor or a potter, it doesn't matter. I try to solve problems.

This is an extract from an article in the *Ceramic Review* by Mo Jupp

'Standing Female' by Mo Jupp, height 5'10".
Red clay and white slip, made in three sections, fired to 1200°C.

Above
Female forms by Mo Jupp, heights 4″ – 8″.
Porcelain with surface treatment.

Right
Female by Mo Jupp, height 6′.
Made in five sections, white slip and surface colour, fired
to 1100°C.

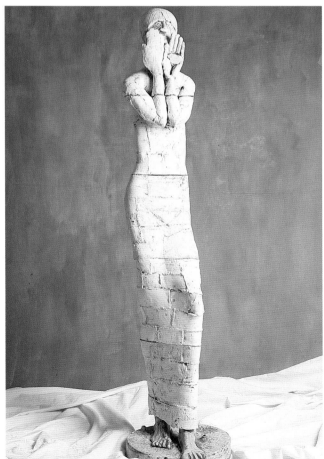

# Ruth Barrett-Danes

The highly expressive and personal works of Ruth Barrett-Danes flourish within the genre of objects that are called ceramics. There are those which are almost indistinguishable from sculpture by reason of great intensity and the submergence of practical function in favour of that of expression. They also do not rely on the innate technical qualities and physical attractiveness of the material and its handling for their aesthetic. If anything they are actively and aggressively devoid of superficial tactile qualities preferring to elevate subject above formal considerations and favouring a narrative exploration of relationships. These are unverifiable and have to be taken on the authority of the maker, her consistancy and deliberation with their metamorphoses are mapped out in clay, colourants and firings. Ruth Barrett-Danes provides the surroundings of a coast line not explored in any medium and those who did are distinguished by the isolated nature of their interests and the unusualness of appropriate metaphors.

Her very earliest influences were those of Arthur Rackham's illustrations, followed by the trenchant work of Gustave Dore and the closed worlds of Hieronymous Bosch and Peter Brueghel. The sinuosities and solipsistic world of calligraphy, monastic illumination and their attendant Bestiaries formed more strata of highly formative experience leading into a realm of fantasy and a concretisation of the radically unfamiliar. A three-dimensional embodiment of that grouping of interests was found in Romanesque architecture and strengthened the essentially linear disciplines of lettering, life drawing, modelling and graphic arts of lithography, etching and wood engraving which her training had laid down.

Later experimentation with imagery derived from fungi and reptilian sources gave a secure vocabulary of forms which were estranged from everyday experience and psychologically potent. Theses cabbage kingdoms and armchair struggles and their implications of claustrophobia are now the archaeological footing of her current productions. Ted Hughes's 'Crow', Blake and T.S. Eliot's wry views helped the for-

'Reptilian Vessel' by Ruth Barrett-Danes, 18 cm.

'Springing Pig' by Ruth Barrett-Danes, height 28 cm.

'Dancing Contest' by Ruth Barrett-Danes, height 34 cm.

mation of clearer personal views and their growth required more flexible expression than the thrown forms permitted and forced a technical reevaluation. The incipient introspection of her profile found a reflection in Virginia Woolf's 'A room of one's own' and may account for the direction of her own interpretations of the subjects and sources of her works. The earlier pieces were predator pots and the first creature in them was a web footed toad who lived in the Abergavenny house and obligingly sat for hours to be drawn. These soft forms gave way to a more muscular and dominant animal which, seemingly trapped by the spherical forms in which it was enclosed, became progressively more aggressive. It developed a beak which it used to free itself by destroying its container. In doing so it destroyed itself. There is a parallel between the development of these expressive forms and the making process in that the pot began as a thrown structure which was later softened to allow the form of the animal to assert

its physical presence. This was then stiffened up, modelled and carved. The sole colour was inlaid colour in the head and the only glaze the lustred eye. These themes represented in the work of recent years have grown from the juxtaposition between man and animal and their innate qualities. The work contains a vision of life as emergent and engulfing, being born and reabsorbed, struggling to be and the protesting against the return to NOT being.

By containing the development of these ideas within an accessible genre, that of the vessel or hollow form, the metamorphic and evolutionary movement from man to animal and vice versa becomes trapped and enveloped, victor and victim becoming one. The work contains private yet universal mythologies harking back to Ovid, the bestiaries and acknowledges Romanesque sculpture, examples of which abound in the countryside where the studio is based.

Extracts from an article by Malcolm Cook

## Paul Astbury

My approach to clay is that of a fine artist. Its plasticity and lack of form compel me to model it. In doing so I discover how transitionery this elementary substance is. Its performance is likened to that of the ancient Greek sea god Proteus' metamorphosis into many shapes and disguises to walk the earth. The very nature of clay is a contradiction. It appears to be easily destroyed, but it is of a nature which also allows it to be reassembled provided the pieces can be found. It is this contrary nature suggesting instability yet permanence which attracts me. Coming from the earth as it does clay seems to echo the transient permanency of nature, within its own mutability. This echo I try to amplify in my work.

In part, this is searched for by using the clay with other materials such as cardboard, paper, tape, ink, oil paint etc. The nature of these is even more vulnerable and impossible to reassemble once their structures are undone. Stronger materials are also used such as wood, metal, plastic etc. Basically these are longer lasting materials, but as is consistent with many other structures they suffer from molecular breakdown eventually.

This leaves the clay suspended amongst these structures relying upon their form and lifetime as a matrix of support for any given shape or arrangement.

I feel it is important to retain these considerations of structure, time and durability while working on the final clay surface. For this reason, I work with inks and paints on many of the clay surfaces once fired to 1260°C. I also used machine oil and emery cloth to smooth the clay, but also to form a residue from these two ingredients which settles within the fine textures and marks on the clay. I rarely use glaze or oxides as they are not immediate enough and usually hide too much of the clay surface. The clay is usually fired to 1260°C.
Clay has no discipline. It has no order to say that it cannot be this or that. It is a three-dimensional brush stroke which has a power to transform, metamorphise with the whim and quickness of mind. It can be made to look like any shape, take on any appearance or quality. It does not force any particular discipline upon the artist. It is free.

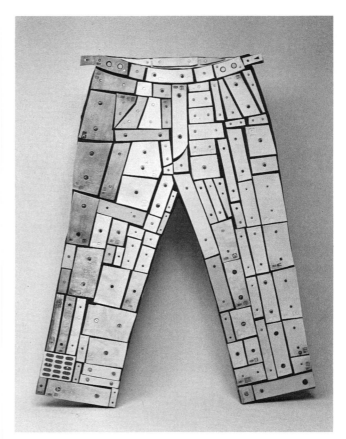

'Work Trousers' by Paul Astbury, 107 × 84 × 7 cm. Porcelain clay, cloth, wood, oil and metal.

When clay is a pot it is within its own domain. Nothing else can make a pot well enough. Clay in sculpture is not there because of this reason, it is there because the artist has said it should be.

Clay opposes discipline in other materials. It is an opposite. It is more like mind and matter combined. Anything malleable is so much more vulnerable to the whims and wishes of the mind that anything which is not. Clay imitates the malleability of the mind. It transforms dreams into actuality. Clay has no real structure, but relies on mind to form it and give it structure. It is this formlessness which has contributed to the fact that there is no school of thought or a movement with a common aim. Artists who use it have been allowed to retain their individuality of approach. Their own common bond being the usage of clay. It is entirely each artist's responsibility to know why he or she uses clay in their work. Probably there is an overall common reason.

It may be that all are attracted by the lack of discipline imposed, and how each one comes to understand this.

'Retread' by Paul Astbury,
61 × 61 × 21 cm.
Assembled mixed media of
car tyre, porcelain, and paper.

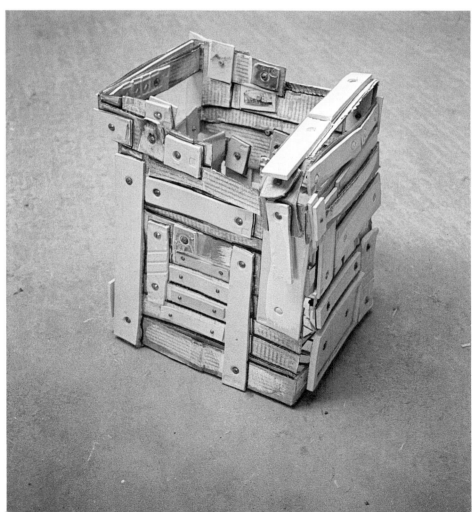

'Reform' by Paul Astbury
2′ × 1′3″ × 1′2″.
Clay and cardboard box.

# Peter Simpson

*Time present and time past*
*are both perhaps present in time future,*
*And time future contained in time past.*
*If all time is eternally present,*
*All time is unredeemable.*

So, at least, T.S. Eliot is not absolutely clear that Peter Simpson would agree with him. Certainly he has been preoccupied with time, or more precisely the evidence of time, since he was a child goggle-eyed at the magical jumble of the old-fashioned local museum. There fossils and birds' eggs and shards of Roman pottery and stuffed animals and bits of carved stone and wood from the Middle Ages would cluster under one roof, with more obvious relationship to the Renaissance wunderkammer than to the neatly signposted educational facilities of today. Yet curiously enough, this very clutter often inspired in the right children (of whom Simpson was one) a serious interest in archaeology and other more systematic ways of understanding the intricate palimpsest of our life and in our own time. Yes, all time is eternally present, but still time can be redeemed and re-examined piece by piece to see how everything fits together.

Such thoughts have informed Simpson's work right from the start. He was trained as a sculptor, and always felt that in choosing to work in ceramics he was simply making a choice of materials, not confining himself to some particular ghetto. And feeling as he did, obviously the message – what his pots were if you like, about – was always going to take precedence over and be served by the medium. Of course the qualities of the specific materials he chose to use in any given case were vitally important, but they were chosen in the light of their suitability for saying what he had to say and not *vice versa*. And right from the beginning what he had to say had a lot to do with the extraordinary and mysterious hidden at the heart of the ordinary and everyday. The porcelain pieces by which he first became well known all took something or-

ganic as the starting point for their imagery: the seed-head of a poppy, a pomegranate split open, the underside of a mushroom, some plant-like animal of the rock pool. Everyday enough, and yet rendered extraordinary and replete with hidden meaning by the intensity of Simpson's gaze, his way of abstracting and generalizing through extreme particularity.

But he did not stay for long with the re-examination, however selective and intense, in nature. His slow-burning interest in the archaeology of ancient Egypt and Pre-Columbian America, not to mention the ritual stones of the English countryside was somewhere present even in the very earliest pieces, since by taking ideas from these natural forms he was, consciously or unconsciously revisiting the primeval sources of design. In the works that followed, more evidently sculptural, more clearly removed from direct representation of any kind, these references came to the surface to create a web of ritual associations. There were first the 'Baton' pieces, in which the form of an animal jawbone appears. Anyone brought up in the western Judeo-Christian tradition is likely to start thinking at once of biblical combats involving the jawbone of an ass. Habitués of archaeological and ethnographic museums will be instantly aware of all the practical and religious uses to which the bones of animals could be put. And for those who were of an age to thrill to Kubrick's film *2001* there is the unforgettable image of the apes' first instruction in the use of bones as tools and weapons by the basalt teaching machine from outer space.

Extract from an article by J. Russel-Taylor

My pieces are made by using some or all of the following methods and techniques.

'Souvenirs de Carcassonne' by Peter Simpson, height 69 × 76 × 26 cm.

Body stain, underglaze, fired to 1240°C. Wax polish and lacquer.
Photographed by Nickolas Gossip.

## Methods and Techniques

White stoneware handbuilding body. Porcelain body, White engobe, Press moulded, Slab built/coil, Thrown, Modelled/carved. Biscuit 1000° centigrade, Underglaze, body stain, biscuit slip, Stoneware 1240° centigrade multi-fired, Barium glazes, Acrylic pigments, Lacquers, stains, waxes and polish.

The sections pinned together using aluminium rod sleeved with aluminium tube, cemented into place with resin.

I believe working methods and techniques, the size of kiln, one's patterns of work etc. must in some way 'edit' one's ideas and by doing so also become influential. Surely one selects the medium knowingly: ceramic has tremendous potential, is incredibly versatile, of course it imposes certain restrictions and conditions: but these too may be seen as positive factors. Technique is not unimportant for me but it is a secondary consideration. The idea comes first and processes that will help to progress the idea are then 'bolted on'. The work is not process led – it is ideas led.

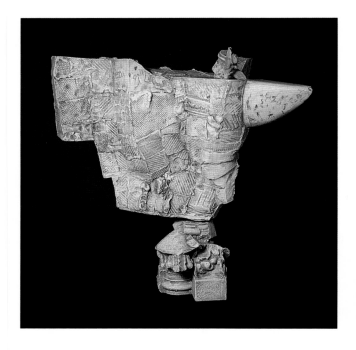

Top right
'Gris Charentais' by Peter Simpson, 65 × 68 × 50 cm.
Body stain and underglaze. Fired to 1240°C.
Photographed by Nickolas Gossip.

Right
'Croix Rouge' by Peter Simpson, height 93 × 74 × 33 cm.
Body stain, underglaze. Alkaline glazes, 1240°C.
Photographed by Nickolas Gossip.

Right
'Romanesque Graffiti' by Peter Simpson, 55 × 70 × 33 cm.
Underglaze; alkaline glaze fired to 1240°C. Polished with wet/dry paper and wax polished.

## David Suckling

One of the opportunities that handbuilding ceramic forms offers me is the freedom of combining my training in both sculpture and painting. The growth of the object in wet clay enables the life force in a work to develop through meditation upon the form. An unlocking of a subconscious way of thinking seems to take over and strongly dictate the direction the piece will take.

The clay body that I use is a buff coloured raku mixed with sand which is well suited to the way in which I work and very tolerant to misuse.

I have a palette of colours which includes basic earthenware glazes, coloured slips and engobes. I use oxides and commercial stains to obtain a further range mixed with glazes such as barium and calcium bases. Some pieces are re-worked with oil paints to obtain the exact finishes that I require. The initial firing is at bisque temperature and after decorating with a basic design in engobe and other materials the piece is fired again at 1080°C.

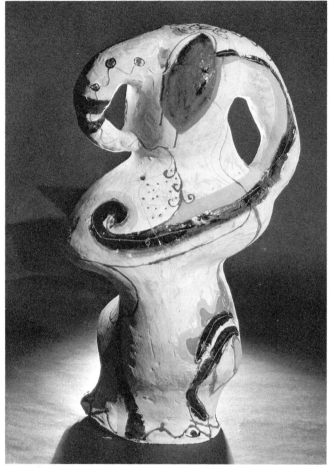

Above
'Channelling the Moon' by David Suckling, height 82 cm.

Page 137 left
'Untitled' by David Suckling, height 121 cm.

Page 137 right
'Primitive Groove' by David Suckling, height 100 cm.

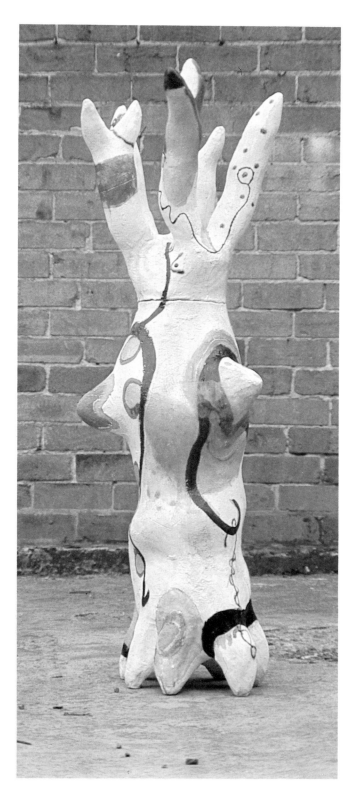
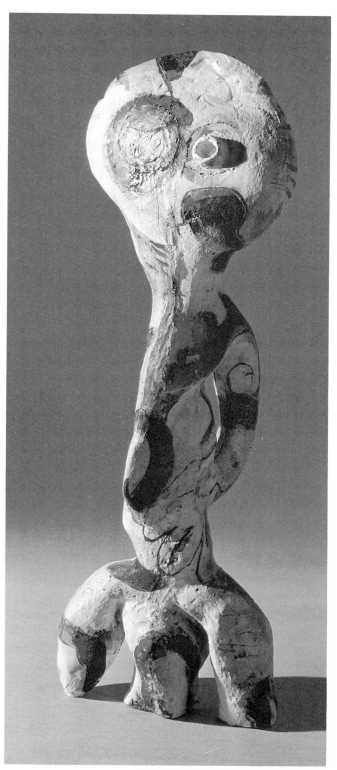

# Michael Flynn

In the past I have tried to indicate the nature of the thoughts underlying my work. One exhibition was titled 'Themes of Love and Death'. Whilst this may have revealed some of the spiritual and romantic elements I considered important, it did not embrace those qualities of ambiguity and humour I also felt to be essential. I therefore tried later to further clarify my intent by referring to Schopenhauer. 'Life is always tragic, but in its isolated details it has the character of a farce.'

More recently Milan Kundera has described the European novel as an 'art born of the laughter of god'. A description which expresses succinctly the goal towards which I strive. I am engaged in an activity which is necessarily a synthesis of such ambition: on the other hand imagery gleaned from observed situations, photography, music, dance, theatre and especially literature, and on the other, my particular fascination with ceramic processes, the qualities derived therefrom and their combination with sculptural considerations. Concern with the relationship of surface and colour to form has lead to bronze casting and patination which offer an interesting equivalent to ceramics.

Trotsky wrote that 'The creative union of the conscious with the unconscious is what one usually calls inspiration'. I have so far referred only to those conscious elements which inform my practice – the starting point, underlying choice of motif and the merging of disparate elements, is more difficult to identify. I must however acknowledge at least three important facts in my life: an Irish Catholic unbringing, an early childhood in Germany and a deep though somewhat removed love of farm life.

If art is not to be neutralised into a mere conveyor or illustrator of other people's truths or some sort of service area in support of one dogma or the other the artist must find his own path. A true work of art is invariably about itself. Its value relies upon the aesthetic of its own emergence and in the possibilities it opens up to its audience. Although my own concern is with

'Harlequin' by Michael Flynn. Raku and brick.

'The 5th Ride' by Michael Flynn, height 22".
Raku.

the visual arts, I am again moved to quote Milan Kundera who uses words far more efficiently that I do: 'If instead of seeking the poem hidden somewhere behind, the poet engages himself to the service of truth known from the outset . . . he has renounced the mission of poetry. It matters little whether the preconceived truth is called revolution or dissidence, Christian faith or atheism, whether it is more or less justified; a poet who serves any truth other than the truth to be discovered is a false poet.'

This is my attempted, albeit clumsily and rather too dryly, effort to unveil the often conflicting, frequently elusive ideas, questions, fears, hopes and ambitions which result in my finished work; or indeed at times stops me from producing anything at all. Yet having stated this I believe that the object must in the end exist for itself: that its starting point is really only of relevance to me, that it should be divested of meaning, that it begs new meaning. One final quotation, this time from Josef Skvorecky, 'Art captures that essence which reality, sometimes more, sometimes less, spreads thin. In art, the essence presents itself as an undiluted, powerful possibility. And because art incarnates what is possible, it can mean anything under the sun.'

*Alan Barrett-Danes states . . .*
'Michael Flynn's figures and animals are a means of expressing his thoughts and he tries to indicate the nature of his thoughts by the titles he gives to individual pieces of work.

The clownishness and sexual elements contained within the human figure and its relationship with the animal mirror one another. The raw physical energy that transmits between man and animal evokes a throbbing unity of like-souls. It is a spirited feeling of escape from the limitation of one's earthly lot.

The influences and autobiographical experiences that feed indirectly into the work are many and varied. Literature, especially mythology, ancient or modern, often provides a catalyst for the development and realisation of ideas alone with elements from the observed situations of music and drama.

Flynn's sculptures possess a powerful visual dynamic, and a dramatic intensity derived from the inherent understanding and qualities of the media used in their making.'

'The Idea' by Michael Flynn, height 35 cm. Raku.

'God for a Happy Home'
by Michael Flynn,
earthenware, 48" high.

'Catching the Cock' by
Michael Flynn, height 16".
Raku, glazed and fired.

# Donna Polseno

'The desire to express aspects of the universality of the human experience, like the ability to adapt, survive and find one's own sense of power in the face of adversity, has been of primary importance to my recent clay work.

Several years ago, I was striving for a liveliness and sense of motion in the vessel form through the use of colour relationships, overlapping patterns and asymmetrical form, tending to use the human form as inspiration. The historic relationship between pottery and the figure, neck, foot and belly suited my intention of taking this symbolic reference as far as possible. Having always worked in an intuitive way rather than conceptually I began by exaggerating these figures, without actually deciding to do so, embuing them with life and energy. They quickly blossomed into forms like voluptuous fertility goddesses. These archetypal figures were meant to contain, protect and nourish the life spirit. Exaggerating the torso was a way of expressing the uniqueness of the life-giving qualities of the female form.

One of the ways that I have personalized this archetypal image is by the exaggeration of movement which is the antithesis of the historical fertility goddess usually represented in a stiff earthbound, immobile pose. My figures contradict this norm expressing the tenuousness of life in motion combined with voluptuousness. I deal with these concerns on a physical as well as an emotional level simultaneously. The forms are built using coils of white earthenware which allow time to articulate the envisioned shape and movement. Once built the clay is further developed with a thick coat of slip brushed over the surface sometimes in a swirling motion. This texture helps to draw the eye and create another visual depth before further surface treatments are added. Above all my pieces develop a sense of being and are not just a reference to the physical body.'

Extract from article in *Ceramics Monthly* (USA) by Donna Polseno

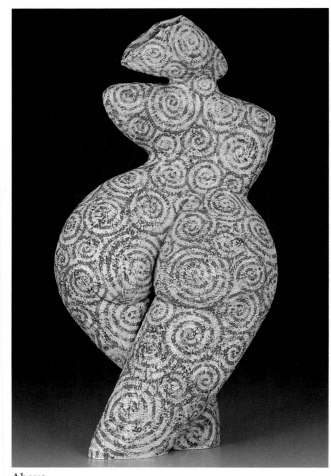

Above
Figure by Donna Polseno, height 27".
Coil built earthenware with stained slips and flux.

Right
Untitled figure by Donna Polseno, height 38".
Earthenware, coiled, slips and stains and flux.

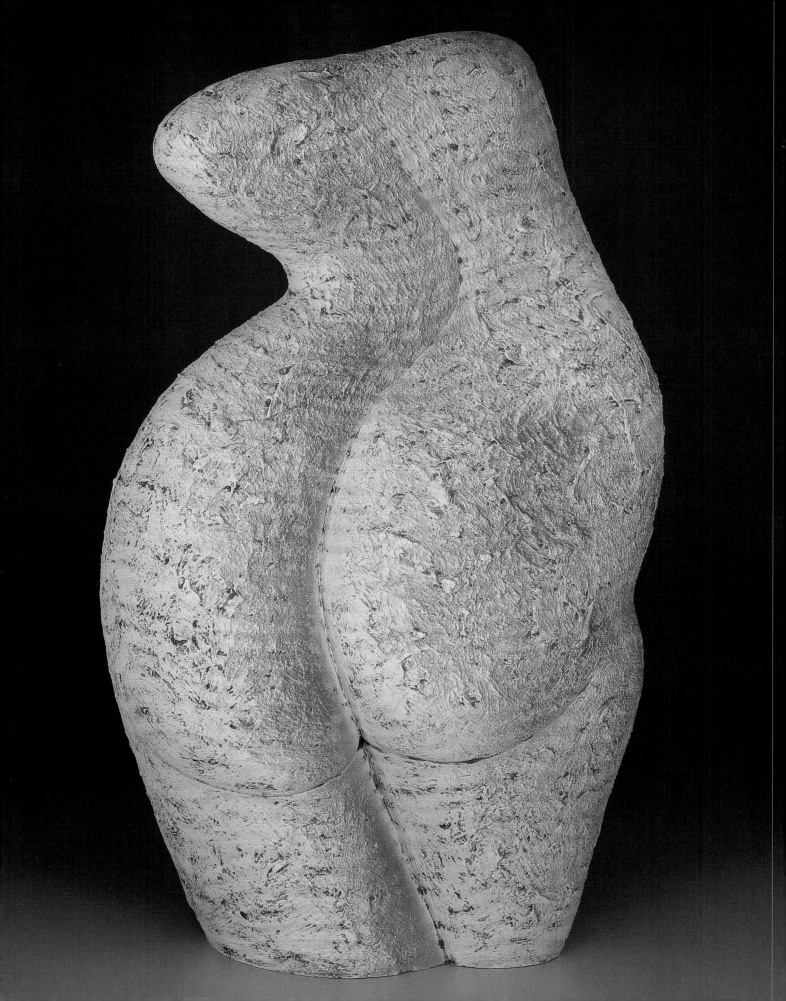

## Vincent McGrath

The driving force of McGrath's work has been his attempts to come artistically to terms with the nature of the Australian environment and in particular the impact of European man on the landscape. This has evolved from earlier concerns relating to more functionally orientated forms. His earliest sculptural ceramics and murals attempted to 'reflect and expand on the form, shape pattern, as well as the visual and tactile textures associated with the elements of nature'. Through a successive development of theme and form, McGrath's work has achieved a maturity and confidence demonstrated by his utilisation of clay as a plastic element of construction and expression.

Through a successive development of theme and form, his work has achieved a maturity and confidence demonstrated by his utilisation of clay as a plastic element of construction and expression.

'My earlier work relied a great deal on effect through the execution of sophisticated clay process methods. I realised that the scale of the pieces was a limitation, the techniques often superficial and the work in general nothing more than a clay exercise. The objects did not communicate anything about contemporary life or address themselves to a lasting beauty. When I was commissioned to undertake three major installation pieces, my thinking towards clay as an expressive medium altered radically. I found that clay responded more sympathetically when it is worked instinctively and intuitively. As the scale of the pieces increased I found the medium became more accommodating, more responsive and more forgiving.'

The resolution of these new directions through an altered approach to methods of production and a focusing of conceptual objectives, is demonstrated by the developments in McGrath's work from simple graphic slab platters to complex three-dimensional enclosed sculptural forms which incorporated varying degrees of scale and applications of personal descriptive imagery.

'I consider my work to be in a state of flux. It is a continual progression of conceptual thinking rather than a change in method or expressive vocabulary. The means by which the statement is made is always changing to suit the expression . . . I am never dictated to by a process just because I am comfortable with it.'

These are extracts from an article by Glenda King, Queen Victoria Museum and Art Gallery

Right
'The Steps of Beaconsfield' by Vincent McGrath, 54 × 24 × 57 cm.
Earthenware, low-fired glazes, underglaze stains and body stains.

Left
'Relic I' by Vincent McGrath, 42 × 18 × 28 cm.
This piece is made from handbuilding raku clay made up into hand slabs. Applied slips are very thick with the addition of earthenware glazes. Once fired at 1150°C.

# Laurie Spencer

Laurie Spencer gained inspiration for her domed structures from her keen interest in insect nests and their complex structures. The 'Imarets', meaning a hostel for the pilgrims on their way to Mecca, have been built in varying sizes. The main structure measures some 15 feet in height. Previous works were concerned with constructing clay works that produced sounds. Many of these whistles developed her interest in the natural acoustics of an enclosed space and how this in turn affected the tone and spiritual quality of pitch and intensity of sound. The development of the domes which are built from rolled coils began with small structures and on to the 'Imaret', built from 7 tonnes of clay, a body of one part buff clay, one part red clay and one part sand reinforced with hay. The catenary arch design helps to keep the structure stable as the work progresses. Due to the weight of material there still remains the need to keep the walls supported by buttresses and this is achieved by a wooden teepee-shaped former built inside, which also acts as a platform in order to reach the upper parts of the clay walls as the height increases. Bags of straw are also used to help create the form and in padding between the wooden framework allowing the clay walls to contract as they dry.

Once completed the entire structure is wrapped in a ceramic fibre blanket and this is then covered in aluminium foil to help retain and reflect the heat. The doors and windows are temporarily bricked to help seal the structure during firing. Passages are then dug in the ground to provide extra air to the two stoke holes and their grates before the fires are set and the firing commences. Interior baffles direct the heat up the walls and down to two flue holes at ground level that are then vented in turn up through the top of the dome in order to reach an optimum temperature of 2000°F. Additional oxygen is supplied to the fire boxes by two gas powered leaf blowers allowing for more complete combustion of the wood within the structure.

Extract from *Ceramics Monthly* by
David Proeber USA

Above
'Hydropolyp' by Laurie Spencer, 22½″ × 10″ × 10½″.
Ceramic whistle.

Left
Untitled Hut by Laurie Spencer, 8′ × 10′.

Below
Imaret by Laurie Spencer, 14′ × 12′.
Coil built, domed structure.

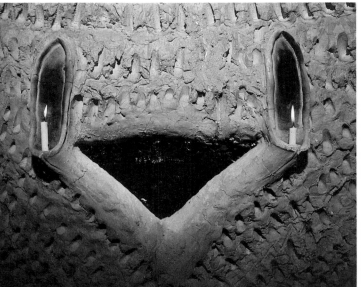

Above
Imaret interior by Laurie Spencer.

# Barbara Tipton

Having travelled Europe and worked in ceramics, Barbara has set up her workshop in Calgary in Canada. In the past she was always attracted to sites of human habitation, or worship and congregation. Her experiences of living in Bath and London in Great Britain, both of which were once old Roman cities as well as now modern urban cultures helped sow the seeds of ideas of the type of works that she began to design. Added to this her visits to sites like Bath Abbey which was a single structure built on the site of an old church which had in its turn been built over an old pagan ritual ground had further profound effects. There were other places too, a quiet church in Derbyshire and the spatial power of Wells Cathedral. On her return to the studio in Canada she became absorbed with images of early English stone sculpture and architecture, and sought to realise them through drawing. This medium allows her ideas to become crystallised and the ceramics to grow out of a response to the atmosphere created by this visualisation of form.

'Fragments IV' (Boat/shelf) by Barbara Tipton, 72 × 22 × 10 cm.
Slab constructed stoneware boat/shelf, press moulded and broken lion head thinly rolled porcelain figure pressed and broken onto freshly glazed bisque. Fired to cone 6 in oxidation.

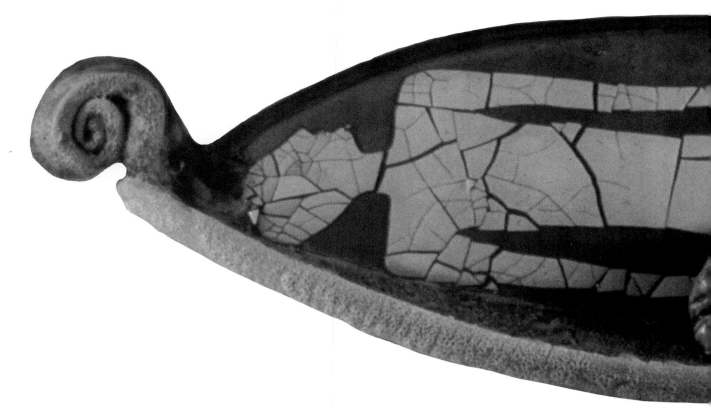

Detail of 'Fragments IV'.

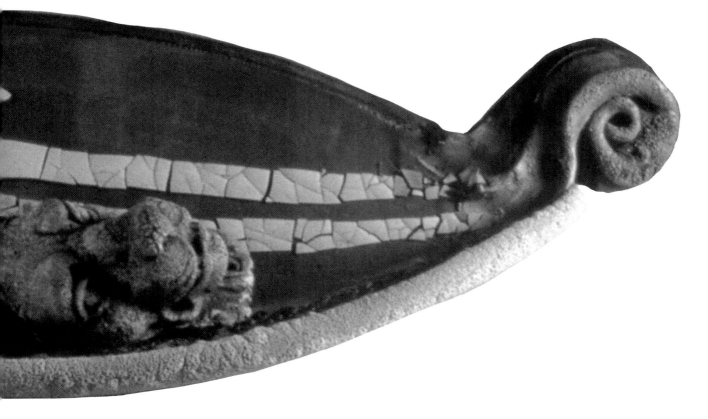

# Health Notes on Toxic Materials

There are a great number of materials that can have dangerous effects on the individual when used in many of the processes involved in the production of ceramics. Some can cause pulmonary disorders through the inhalation of dust, clay particles and other airborne materials. Many of these materials are not poisonous in themselves and are benign and inert, but due to their very fine particle size can easily be drawn into the lungs. China clay for example if inhaled over an extended period can cause silicosis. Fine silica dust is known to be the principal cause of this problem and although in many cases it can take years of exposure to the materials, it can also happen in a matter of months. Those who suffer from asthmatic and other respiratory complaints should never under any circumstances be exposed to these airborne materials or to others like gum arabic that have been known to produce the symptoms of asthma in some people.

Alumina can induce a disease that is called aluminosis. Very similar to silicosis, this too is caused by inhaling particles of the material in question.

Fibreglass and asbestos particles can be very dangerous. Both can cause irritation to the skin and induce cancerous growths when the particles are drawn into the lungs.

Siderosis is a problem brought on by the inhalation of iron oxide.

There are many other materials that can be the cause of illness so it is essential that a mask should always be worn when working with powdered materials of any kind.

Fine airborne particles are not the only serious danger in the workshop or studio. There are others that can be poisonous to the system either by direct ingestion as well as through absorption and contact through the skin. Almost all lead compounds for example, with the exception of some fritted varieties, are poisonous. Antimony can cause dermatitis and conjunctivitis. The list is very large and some of the more dangerous materials are listed below.

*Barium* can cause muscular paralysis.

*Borax* can bring on convulsions.

*Cadmium* can cause choking and vomiting.

*Cobalt* can induce dermatitis.

*Lithium* can affect the kidneys.

*Manganese* is poisonous and can cause drowsiness and loss of function.

*Nickel* affects the skin, causing possible dermatitis.

*Silica* mentioned before can induce symptoms of silicosis.

*Selenium* is very poisonous and also brings on skin problems.

*Talc, uranium salts* and other materials such as *vanadium* attack the respiratory tract as well as the lungs.

There can be other problems caused when metallic oxides are released from fired glazes when they are used for domestic purposes in the storage of food and drink. There are regulations that cover the use of some of these materials for production ware. The most serious and more common problem is the release of lead from glazes. The use of lead frit in any mix does not always remove the danger. The combination of copper oxide can in some cases act as a catalyst and allow the lead released by the glaze to exceed the recommended limits for safe use. Glazes containing these supposedly safe additives are also able to release greater amounts of toxic agents if they are not fired to maturity when all the components are fused together and sealed against possible infusion with other materials. The storage of acidic fruit juices and pickled vegetables mixed with vinegar are particularly able to leech these materials out of the glaze and react with them. If in any doubt always have any lead glazed containers tested in a laboratory situation that understands the current legislation for their safe use.

To return to the problems in a studio situation, care must always be taken when sweeping the floor and bench tops. These will have the residual remains of various working activities still on them both from the making and glazing processes. When sweeping the ensuing dust can be full of toxic materials. Always wear a mask when engaged in this activity however tedious it may seem at the time. There are several recommended respirators available. In America they are approved under the heading of NIOSH, in Canada WHMIS and covered by the Factory Inspection Act in Great Britain. Spraying should never be carried out in a confined space and if possible always with some method of extraction of the materials away from the user in the way of a spray booth. Take the added precaution of wearing a mask even if there are adequate facilities for the dispersal of airborne particles.

Apart from the use of these materials and the avoidance of ill health from their use in the studio, there are one or two final points which should be considered. They have been mentioned earlier in the text on kilns but are well worth noting again.

Never leave combustible materials near the firing area and always ensure that all the kiln equipment is in good order between each firing. Always wear gloves to protect the hands when the firing is in progress and if possible, goggles that are graded to the appropriate temperature when looking through spy holes to observe the cones and conditions within the chamber. Try and avoid the inhalation of gases that are emitted from the kiln at all stages of the firing cycle however innocuous they may seem. Remember that even the homely garden bonfire can emit deadly carcinogenic and poisonous gases.

Always treat studio machinery with respect and remember that it has the potential to cause injury. Never carry out repairs with out disconnecting the power supply nor be tempted to put a hand into mixing or milling machines under any circumstances.

Finally, never eat or smoke when handling any of the materials mentioned above and wash thoroughly after the work is finished. As a last safety measure, keep a good first aid kit and a fire extinguisher available at all times.

Above
Vase by Anna Lambert, height 7".
Waves and mackerel decoration.

Below
'Nuts & Bolts' by Delan Cookson, height 30 cm.
Ash glazed stoneware.

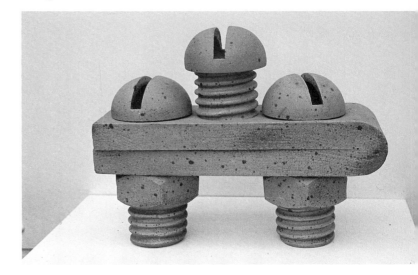

151

# Clay Recipes:

## From Donna Polseno

### Earthenware Body
#### (Cone 04)

| | |
|---|---|
| Talc | 30lbs. |
| Ball Clay | 30 |
| Cedar Heights | |
|     Goldart Clay | 100 |
| Medium Grog | 25 |
| | 185lbs. |

Dry mix this body with one handful of nylon fibres.

### Porcelain Casting Slip
#### (Cone 7)

| | |
|---|---|
| Custer Feldspar | 18lbs. |
| Frit 3110 (Ferro) | 2 |
| Nepheline Syenite | 70 |
| Ball Clay | 50 |
| Edgar Plastic Kaolin | 36 |
| 6 Tile Clay | 10 |
| Flint | 14 |
| | 200lbs. |

Add 356 grams of sodium silicate to $10\frac{1}{2}$ gallons of water before mixing with the dry ingredients.

### Pebbly Slip
#### (Cone 7)

| | |
|---|---|
| Borax | 4.31% |
| Opax | 6.68 |
| Talc | 12.93 |
| Tin Oxide | 2.59 |
| Frit 3110 (Ferro) | 24.35 |
| Ball Clay | 12.07 |
| Edgar Plastic Kaolin | 20.26 |
| Flint | 16.81 |
| | 100.00% |

Spray this slip for a dry, pebbly surface.

## From David Miller

### Raku Body Mix
plastic

50 kilos white burning refractory fire clay (none)
20 kilos white earthenware clay (plastic)
15 kilos talc
20 kilos coarse grog (0.5 to 1 mm)
10 kilos fine chamotte (0.2 to 0.5 mm)

### Handbuilding clay

50 kilos white burning refractory clay
10 kilos white earthenware clay
15 kilos talc
40 kilos coarse grog

Both of these mixes are good for raku and low temperature salting and are resistant to thermal shock.

### Raku Glaze
White opaque crackle glaze

70 parts borocalcite frit
10 parts soft alkaline frit
20 parts ball clay
10% tin oxide

This glaze is painted on thinly over parts of the decoration to create a sort of resist against the reduction. The colours remain brighter and are in contrast to the darker matt surroundings.

### Vitreous Slip

8.75 borocalcite frit
1.25 alkaline frit
20    quartz or flint
40    China clay

When adding high temperature colour stains, they should modified with the addition of 25% alkaline frit. This is important otherwise the colours will not adhere to the surface. The slip is applied thinly after the bisque firing at 1000°C but before the stains and glaze are added.

**Stoneware glazes**

Matt white

> Barium carbonate 50%
> China clay 50%

Clear base glaze

| | |
|---|---|
| Talc | 12 |
| Potash feldspar | 32 |
| Whiting | 14 |
| China clay | 8 |
| Quartz | 34 |

This glaze can be opacified or coloured in the usual manner and has a rich fluid surface.

A simple shino glaze

| | |
|---|---|
| Nepheline syenite | 33 |
| Feldspar | 33 |
| Ball clay | 33 |

Petalite instead of nepheline syenite lowers the firing temperature. This is a good all round stoneware glaze, buttery in texture, takes stains well and can be used as a raw glaze or on bisque ware.

'Garden' maquette for monument by Michael Flynn, height 14".

# *Recipes for Casting Slips*

(kindly provided by clay suppliers)

| | | weight of dry clay | water | soda ash | sodium silicate 140°TW |
|---|---|---|---|---|---|
| Cedar Heights Redart Clay 1800°–2000°F | | 663g | 337cc | 1.4g | 6.4g |
| Harrison Mayer Bone China Body 1240°–1250°C | | 1000g | 450cc | – | 3.3g |
| Harrison Mayer Stoneware Clay 1180°–1250°C | | 1000g | 400cc | – | 4.7g |
| Kentucky–Tennessee 1900°–2200°C | OM 4 Ball Clay | 16 lbs | | | |
| | Tenn 5 Ball Clay | 16 lbs | | | |
| | Whiting | 4 lbs | | | |
| | New York State Talc | 64 lbs | 45 lbs | 1 oz | 6 to 12 oz |
| | Barium Carbonate | up to 1 oz | | | |
| Moira Stoneware Clay 1200°–1240°C | | 1½ cwts | 2½ galls | 3½ oz | 2¾ oz |
| Podmore & Sons David Leach Porcelain 1200°–1280°C | | 5000g | 2960cc | – | 9.9cc |
| Podmore & Sons Red Terracotta Clay 1100°–1160°C | | 5000g | 1900cc | 13.9g | 30.7cc(75°TW) |
| Podmore & Sons White Earthenware Body 1100°–1160°C | | 5000g | 2000cc | 7.1g | 5.5cc |

From *Clays* by Frank Hamer and Janet Hamer (A & C Black)

**Geoffrey Eastops porcelain slip casting recipe:**

| China clay | 13 lb |
| Flint | 4.5 lb |
| Potash feldspar | 7.25 lb |
| BBV ball clay | 3 lb |
| Bentonite | 0.5 lb |
| Sodium silicate 140°TW | 32 gm |
| Water | 12 pints |

**Gillian Lowndes casting slip**
given by Scott Chamberlain (USA)

| Grolleg China clay | 660 lb |
| Feldspar | 300 lb |
| Flint | 240 lb |
| Sodium silicate | 2 lb |
| Dispex | 1 lb |
| Water | 1 pint |

Gillian uses this to soak fibreglass tissue in for some of her work.

**Casting slip used by Ron Burke (USA)**

| Victoria ball clay | 125 lb |
| Jordon stoneware | 50 lb |
| Cedar Heights | 50 lb |
| Fireclay | 100 lb |
| Feldspar | 16 lb |
| Water | 140 lb |
| Deflocculent | 1900 gm |

This is a light burning strong clay.

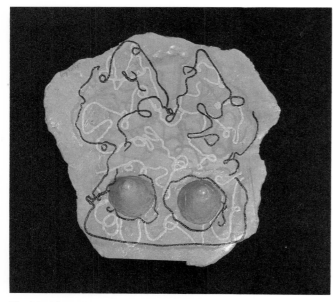

Untitled by Jill Crowley.
Photograph by Stephen Brayne.

# Recipes for Special Bodies

### Egyptian Paste

| Soda feldspar | 40 |
| Flint | 18 |
| China clay no 1 | 15 |
| Ball clay no 4 | 5 |
| Sodium carbonate | 12 |
| Whiting | 5 |
| Fine silver sand no 1 | 8 |
| Bentonite | 2 |

| _Colourings:_ | Copper oxide | 1–3 |
| | Manganese dioxide | 2–3 |
| | Cobalt oxide | 1–2 |
| | Chromium oxide | 1–2 |

First grind together dry ingredients then add only sufficient water to make a stiff paste. During drying the soda crystallizes on the surface where it develops a glaze upon firing to 980°C (1796°F).

### David Leach Translucent Porcelain Body
(Recipe supplied by David Leach)

| Grolleg China clay | 53 |
| Potash feldspar | 25 |
| Fine-ground quartz | 17 |
| Quest white bentonite | 5 |

This body is throwable and is normally fired to 1280°C (2336°F) in reduction. This body was marketed by Podmore & Sons Ltd. David Leach is at present researching an improved composition which will also be marketed by Podmore's.

### Harrison Mayer Bone China Body
(Recipe suplied by Harrison Mayer Ltd)

| Calcined bone | 49 |
| Cornish stone | 25 |
| China clay | 25 |
| Ball clay | 1 |

This body is for casting and jolleying. Firing temperature 1240°C (2264°F).

# Cone Temperature Conversion Table for Staffordshire Cones, Seger Cones and Orton Cones

*NB: Large cones. Squatting temperature depends on rate of firing.*

| °C | °F | Staffs Cones | Seger Cones | Orton Cones |
|---|---|---|---|---|
| 710 | 1310 | 018 | 018 | – |
| 720 | 1328 | – | – | 018 |
| 770 | 1418 | – | – | 017 |
| 790 | 1454 | 015 | 015a | – |
| 815 | 1499 | 014 | 014a | – |
| 830 | 1526 | – | – | 014 |
| 855 | 1571 | 012 | – | – |
| 860 | 1580 | – | 012a | 013 |
| 900 | 1652 | 010 | 011a | – |
| 905 | 1661 | – | – | 011 |
| 940 | 1724 | 08 | 09a | – |
| 950 | 1742 | – | – | 08 |
| 970 | 1778 | – | 07a | 07 |
| 980 | 1796 | 06 | 06a | – |
| 1000 | 1832 | 05 | 05a | – |
| 1015 | 1859 | – | – | 06 |
| 1020 | 1868 | 04 | 04a | – |
| 1040 | 1904 | 03 | – | 05 |
| 1060 | 1940 | 02 | 03a | 04 |
| 1080 | 1976 | 01 | 02a | – |
| 1100 | 2012 | 1 | 01a | – |
| 1115 | 2039 | – | – | 03 |
| 1120 | 2048 | 2 | – | – |
| 1125 | 2057 | – | 1a | 02 |
| 1140 | 2084 | 3 | – | – |
| 1145 | 2093 | – | 2a | 01 |
| 1200 | 2192 | 6 | 4a | – |
| 1205 | 2201 | – | – | 6 |
| 1230 | 2246 | 7 | – | 7 |
| 1250 | 2282 | 8 | – | 8 |
| 1260 | 2300 | 8a | 7 | 9 |
| 1280 | 2336 | 9 | 8 | – |
| 1285 | 2345 | – | – | 10 |
| 1300 | 2372 | 10 | 9 | – |
| 1305 | 2381 | – | – | 11 |
| 1320 | 2408 | 11 | 10 | – |
| 1325 | 2417 | – | – | 12 |
| 1335 | 2435 | – | 11 | 13 |

# UK/USA Substitute Materials

| UK | USA |
|---|---|
| Alkaline leadless frit | Ferro 3110 |
| | Pemco P-991 |
| Ball clay (Hymod SMD) | Kentucky ball clay |
| | Tennessee ball clay |
| Standard borax frit | Ferro 3134 |
| | Pemco P-996 |
| Now available from Potclays Ltd. | Colemanite; Gerstley borate |
| China Clay | EPK Florida; Georgia china; Kaolin |
| Cornish stone, China stone | Cornish stone; Caroline stone; Kona A-3; Pyrophyllite |
| Feldspar (Potash) | Bell, Buckingham G-200; Kingman K-200; Custer; Clinchfield 202 |
| Feldspar (Soda) | Spruce Pine 4; Kona F-4 |
| Fremington clay | Albany slip clay |
| Lead bisilicate | Ferro 3498 |
| | O Hommel 14 |
| | Pemco P6–700 |
| Zirconium silicate (Zircon) (Disperzon) | 'Opax', 'Superpax', 'Zircopax' |

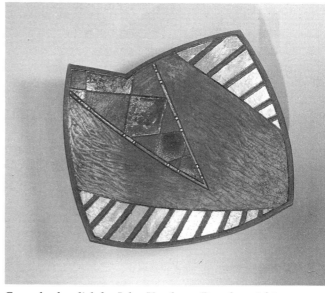

Carved raku dish by John Kershaw. Based on African masks with a geometric representation of the face. Photograph by Andrew Morris.

# *Analyses of Clays*

(Kindly provided by the producers and suppliers)

| | | | | *ultimate analysis* | | | | | | |
|---|---|---|---|---|---|---|---|---|---|---|
| | $SiO_2$ | $TiO_2$ | $Al_2O_3$ | $Fe_2O_3$ | $MgO$ | $CaO$ | $Na_2O$ | $K_2O$ | *loss* | |
| *English China Clays* | | | | | | | | | | |
| Standard Porcelain China Clay | 47.2 | 0.05 | 37.4 | 0.6 | 0.2 | 0.2 | 0.1 | 1.7 | 12.3 | |
| Grolleg China Clay | 47.7 | 0.03 | 37.2 | 0.7 | 0.25 | 0.1 | 0.1 | 1.95 | 12.06 | |
| Hymod TLD Ball Clay | 55.0 | 1.3 | 30.0 | 1.3 | 0.5 | 0.3 | 0.5 | 3.2 | 8.7 | |
| Hymod SMD Ball Clay | 65.0 | 1.4 | 23.0 | 1.0 | 0.4 | 0.2 | 0.4 | 2.4 | 6.8 | |
| *Moira Pottery* | | | | | | | | | | |
| Stoneware Clay | 59.7 | 1.6 | 25.55 | 1.44 | | | | | 9.46 | |
| *Podmore & Sons* | | | | | | | | | | |
| David Leach Porcelain Body | 61.4 | 0.06 | 26.35 | 0.58 | 0.33 | 0.31 | 0.77 | 3.8 | 7.03 | |
| *Watts Blake Bearne* | | | | | | | | | | |
| CC China Clay | 46.8 | 0.1 | 37.4 | 0.8 | 0.2 | 0.1 | 0.1 | 1.7 | 12.8 | |
| HVA/R Ball Clay | 62.7 | 1.5 | 24.8 | 0.9 | 0.3 | 0.2 | 0.3 | 2.3 | 7.1 | |
| TWVA Ball Clay | 50.5 | 1.0 | 32.8 | 1.0 | 0.3 | 0.2 | 0.3 | 2.2 | 11.7 | |
| BBV Ball Clay | 71.3 | 1.5 | 18.8 | 0.8 | 0.3 | 0.2 | 0.3 | 1.9 | 4.9 | |
| *Cedar Heights* | | | | | | | | | $P_2O_5$ | *loss* |
| Redart Clay | 64.27 | 1.06 | 16.41 | 7.04 | 1.55 | 0.23 | 0.4 | 4.07 | 0.17 | 4.78 |
| Goldart Clay | 57.32 | 1.96 | 28.5 | 1.23 | 0.22 | 0.08 | | 1.18 | | 9.39 |
| *Firehouse Ceramics* | | | | | | | | | | |
| Hammill & Gillespie Blackbird (Barnard) Clay | 59.7 | 0.67 | 10.87 | 14.65 | 0.75 | 0.27 | 0.12 | 2.04 | *MnO* 3.4 | 7.48 |
| Industrial Mineral Products Albany Slip Clay | 57.64 | 0.4 | 14.66 | 5.2 | 2.68 | 5.78 | 0.8 | 3.25 | | 9.46 |
| *Kentucky–Tennessee* | | | | | | | | | | |
| Old Mine 4 Ball Clay | 53.8 | 1.7 | 30.0 | 0.9 | 0.3 | 0.3 | 0.3 | 1.1 | | 11.8 |
| Tennessee 5 Ball Clay | 53.8 | 1.4 | 28.9 | 0.9 | 0.3 | 0.2 | 0.5 | 1.6 | | 12.4 |
| XX Sagger Ball Clay | 56.7 | 1.7 | 29.2 | 0.7 | 0.3 | 0.5 | 0.3 | 0.9 | | 9.9 |
| *Minnesota Clay* | | | | | | | | | | |
| Plastic Vitrox (PV) | 76.16 | | 12.38 | | | 0.48 | 3.23 | 7.72 | fired analysis | |
| Jordan Stoneware | 67.2 | 1.18 | 20.2 | 1.73 | 0.52 | 0.16 | 0.23 | 2.0 | | 6.7 |
| *Potclays* | | | | | | | | | | |
| Oxidising St. Thomas' Body | 67.7 | 0.84 | 20.05 | 1.91 | 0.36 | 0.43 | 0.31 | 1.42 | | 7.01 |
| Reducing St. Thomas' Body | 69.72 | 0.87 | 18.83 | 2.01 | 0.33 | 0.83 | 0.55 | 0.58 | $Mn_3O_4$ 0.01 | 5.27 |
| Pyropot Toasted Body | 56.63 | 1.42 | 31.76 | 3.46 | 0.74 | 0.59 | 2.26 | 1.78 | | 6.04 |
| Special Stoneware | 61.8 | 0.65 | 26.3 | 1.02 | 0.31 | 0.65 | 0.44 | 1.31 | | 7.62 |
| Smooth Stoneware | 57.0 | 0.82 | 25.0 | 3.9 | 0.58 | 0.55 | 0.25 | 1.8 | $Mn_3O_4$ | 9.8 |
| Red S/E Body | 58.0 | 1.5 | 24.0 | 11.0 | 1.0 | 1.6 | 0.2 | 1.5 | 0.2 | fired analysis |

# List of Suppliers

## United Kingdom

*Clays*

Acme Marls Ltd., Bournes Bank, Burslem, Stoke-on-Trent ST6 3DW

C.H. Brannam Ltd, Litchdon Potteries, Barnstaple, Devon EX32 8ND

Clayglaze Ltd., Talbot Road, Rickmansworth, Herts. WD3 1HW

Deancraft Fahey Ltd., Unit 12, Spedding Road, Fenton Industrial Estate, Stoke-on-Trent ST4 2ST

Ellis & Everard Chemicals Ltd., Star Road, Partridge Green, Horsham, W. Sussex RH13 8RA

English China Clays, John Keay House, St Austell, Cornwall PL25 4DJ

Ferro GB Ltd., Ceramic Division, Nile Street, Burslem, Stoke-on-Trent ST6 2BQ

Fulham Pottery Ltd., 8–10 Ingate Place, London SW8 3NS

Moira Pottery Ltd., Raw Materials Dept., Moira, Burton upon Trent, Staffs. DE12 6DF

Morgan Refractories Ltd., Liverpool Road, Neston, South Wirral, Cheshire L64 3RE

Potclays Ltd., Brickkiln Lane, Etruria, Stoke-on-Trent, Staffs. ST4 7BP

Potterycrafts Ltd., Campbell Road, Shelton, Stoke-on-Trent, Staffs. ST4 4ET

Watts, Blake, Bearne & Co., Park House, Courtney Park, Newton Abbot, Devon TQ12 4PS

## United States of America

Continental Clay Co.,
1101 Stinson Blvd NE,
Minneapolis, MN 55413.
612 331 9332

Miller Clay Pottery Suppliers,
South Hadley, Ma.
800 762 7407

Cedar Height Clay,
P.O. Box 295,
Oak Hill, Ohio.
614 682 7794

Standard Ceramic Supply Co.,
P.O. Box 4435,
Pittsburgh, Pa 15205.
412 276 6333

Above
Plate by Anne Mercer, 18″ × 18″.
Laminated porcelain that has been press moulded.

Below
Raku dish by John Kershaw.
Slab built, black and white decoration.

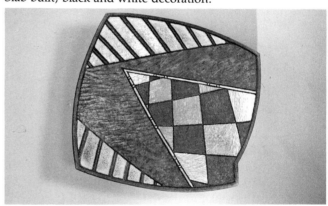

Cinva-Ram Press,
c/o Bellows-Valvair,
200 /est Exchange Street,
Akron, Ohio 44309

Mason Stain Co.,
P.O. Box 76,
East Liverpool, Ohio 43920

Orton Ceramic Foundation,
6991 Old 3c Highway,
Westerville, Ohio

# Further Reading

## Books

Byers, Ian, *Raku* (Batsford).

Clark, Kenneth, *Potters Manual*, (1987).

Colbeck, John, *Pottery Materials* (Batsford).

Cooper, Emmanuel, *A History of World Pottery* (Batsford).

Cooper, Emmanuel and Eileen Lewenstein (eds), *Clay Bodies and Glazes* (Ceramic Review Publications).

Cooper, Emmanuel and Eileen Lewenstein (eds), *Clays and Glazes* (Ceramic Review Publications).

Cooper, Emmanuel and Eileen Lewenstein (eds), *Potters* (Ceramic Review Publications).

Dormer, Peter, *The New Ceramics* (Thames and Hudson).

Flight, Graham, *Ceramics Manual* (Collins).

Fournier, Robert, *The Illustrated Dictionary of Practical Pottery* (A&C Black).

Gregory, Ian, *Kiln Building* (A&C Black).

Lane, Peter, *Ceramic Form* (Collins).

Lane, Peter, *Studio Ceramics* (Collins).

Olsen, Frederick, *The Kiln Book* (A&C Black).

Phillips, Anthony, *Slips and Slipware* (Batsford).

Waller, Jane, *Hand Built Ceramics* (Batsford).

Wren, Rosemary, *Animal Forms and Figures* (Batsford).

Zakin, Richard, *Ceramics: Mastering the Craft* (A&C Black).

## Periodicals

*Ceramics Review*, 21 Carnaby Street, London WW1V 1PH, England.

*Ceramics Monthly*, Box 4548, Columbus, Ohio, USA.

*Crafts Magazine*, Crafts Council, 1 Oxenden Street, London SW1, England.

*Ceramics Art & Perception*, 35 William Street, Paddington, NSW 2021, Australia.

Vessel form by Tina Vlassopulos.
Burnished earthenware.

# INDEX

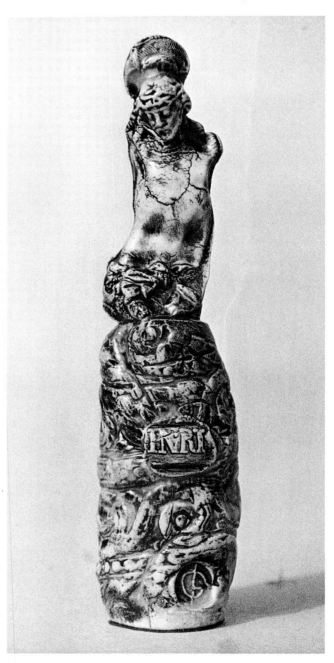

Impressed patterns and letters in porcelain by the Author, 17″ high.